# 30 Day Ketogenic Vegetarian Meal Plan

*Delicious, Easy And Healthy Vegetarian Recipes To Get You Started On The Keto Lifestyle | Lose Weight, Regain Energy And Heal Your Body*

# Table of Contents

Introduction ........................................................................................... 10

What is the ketogenic diet? .................................................................... 11

What does it mean to be vegetarian? .................................................... 11

Benefits of being on both the ketogenic diet and being a vegetarian ............ 12

Foods allowed and not allowed on the ketogenic vegetarian diet .............. 14

30-day meal plan ................................................................................... 20

About these recipes .............................................................................. 20

Day 1 ....................................................................................................... 21

Breakfast ................................................................................................ 21

Cauliflower Cakes ............................................................................... 21

Lunch ...................................................................................................... 22

Leafy Green Salad with Olives, Cheese and Almonds ......................... 22

Dinner ..................................................................................................... 23

Roasted Pumpkin and Cilantro Side Salad .......................................... 23

Day 2 ....................................................................................................... 24

Breakfast ................................................................................................ 24

Eggs and Avocado with Spicy Olive Oil Drizzle ................................. 24

Lunch ...................................................................................................... 26

Asparagus Tart .................................................................................... 26

Dinner ..................................................................................................... 27

Spinach and Leek No-crust Quiche ...................................................... 27

Day 3 ....................................................................................................... 29

Breakfast ................................................................................................ 29

Baked Eggs with Tomato and Basil ..................................................... 29

Lunch ...................................................................................................... 31

"Hot Dogs" with Mustard and Cheese .................................................. 31

Dinner ..................................................................................................... 33

Broccoli, Almond and Feta Salad ........................................................ 33

Day 4 ....................................................................................................... 34

Breakfast .................................................................................... 34

    Brussels Sprout and Zucchini Hash ........................................ 34

Lunch ....................................................................................... 36

    Sesame Seed Sushi (Cucumber, Quinoa, Carrot, Mayo and Sesame Seeds) ............. 36

Dinner ...................................................................................... 37

    Sautéed Spinach and Kale with Halloumi and Fresh Chili ........ 37

Day 5 ........................................................................................ 39

Breakfast .................................................................................. 39

    Green Smoothie .................................................................. 39

Lunch ....................................................................................... 40

    Cheese and Tomato Toasties (with Eggplant Bread) ............... 40

Dinner ...................................................................................... 41

    Tofu and Asparagus Stir Fry ............................................... 41

Day 6 ........................................................................................ 42

Breakfast .................................................................................. 42

    Swiss Chard Omelet ........................................................... 42

Lunch ....................................................................................... 43

    Leek and Feta Salad with Pistachios ................................... 43

Dinner ...................................................................................... 45

    Roasted Zucchini with Garlic Butter and Cauliflower Rice ..... 45

Day 7 ........................................................................................ 47

Breakfast .................................................................................. 47

    Greek Yogurt and Berry Parfait ........................................... 47

Lunch ....................................................................................... 48

    Olive, Red Onion, Cheese and Spinach Salad ...................... 48

Dinner ...................................................................................... 49

    Butternut and Garlic Soup .................................................. 49

Day 8 ........................................................................................ 50

Breakfast .................................................................................. 50

    Pancakes ........................................................................... 50

Lunch ....................................................................................... 52

    Egg and Greens Salad with Yogurt Mint Dressing ............... 52

Dinner ...................................................................................... 54

Cucumber and Tofu Summer Rolls .................................................................54

Day 9 ....................................................................................................................56

Breakfast .............................................................................................................56

Soft-Boiled Eggs with Asparagus Spears ......................................................56

Lunch ...................................................................................................................58

Roasted Veggies with Cheese Balls (Goat Cheese Coated in Seeds) ...........58

Dinner ..................................................................................................................60

Caprese Salad ....................................................................................................60

Day 10 ..................................................................................................................61

Breakfast .............................................................................................................61

Mushroom Muffins ............................................................................................61

Lunch ...................................................................................................................63

Keto Pizza ..........................................................................................................63

Dinner ..................................................................................................................65

Stuffed Zucchinis ..............................................................................................65

Day 11 ..................................................................................................................66

Breakfast .............................................................................................................66

Overnight Oats with Chia and Almond Essence ............................................66

Lunch ...................................................................................................................67

Stuffed Peppers with Mushroom, Goat Cheese and Paprika Filling ............67

Dinner ..................................................................................................................69

Eggplant burgers ...............................................................................................69

Day 12 ..................................................................................................................71

Breakfast .............................................................................................................71

Coconut Coffee Smoothie .................................................................................71

Lunch ...................................................................................................................72

Bok Choy Sesame Stir Fry ................................................................................72

Dinner ..................................................................................................................73

Low-Carb Veggie Curry ....................................................................................73

Day 13 ..................................................................................................................75

Breakfast .............................................................................................................75

Cottage Cheese Hotcakes with Almond Butter ..............................................75

Lunch ...................................................................................................................77

Celery Boats with Nut Butter (Snack) ..............................................77

Dinner .......................................................................................78

Keto Veggie Lasagna ...................................................................78

Day 14 ..........................................................................................80

Breakfast ....................................................................................80

Cauliflower Toast with Avocado ....................................................80

Lunch ........................................................................................82

Fat-bomb Smoothie .....................................................................82

Dinner .......................................................................................83

Grilled Cheese Sandwiches (with Zucchini Bread) ...........................83

Day 15 ..........................................................................................84

Breakfast ....................................................................................84

Keto-Friendly Porridge .................................................................84

Lunch ........................................................................................85

Fried Tempeh Salad .....................................................................85

Dinner .......................................................................................86

Keto Nachos ..............................................................................86

Day 16 ..........................................................................................88

Breakfast ....................................................................................88

Chocolate Bombs ........................................................................88

Lunch ........................................................................................89

Creamy Pesto Pasta (Zoodles) .......................................................89

Dinner .......................................................................................90

Roasted Cauliflower Salad ............................................................90

Day 17 ..........................................................................................91

Breakfast ....................................................................................91

Avocado Berry Smoothie ..............................................................91

Lunch ........................................................................................92

Mac and Cheese (Veggie-Keto Style) ...............................................92

Dinner .......................................................................................94

Quesadillas ...............................................................................94

Day 18 ..........................................................................................96

Breakfast ....................................................................................96

Smoothie Bowl ........................................................................96

Lunch ....................................................................................97

Tomato and Bell Pepper Soup ................................................97

Dinner ...................................................................................98

Fresh, Tangy Slaw ................................................................98

Day 19 .....................................................................................99

Breakfast ...............................................................................99

Keto butter coffee .................................................................99

Lunch ...................................................................................100

Roasted Green Bean and Arugula Salad ..............................100

Dinner ..................................................................................102

Spicy Fried Halloumi with Cabbage and Fresh Chili ...........102

Day 20 ...................................................................................103

Breakfast .............................................................................103

Refreshing Mint, Turmeric and Citrus Smoothie ...............103

Lunch ...................................................................................104

Buddha Bowl with Tofu .......................................................104

Dinner ..................................................................................105

Fresh Salad with Walnut/Avocado Dressing .......................105

Day 21 ...................................................................................107

Breakfast .............................................................................107

Lemon Cheesecake ..............................................................107

Lunch ...................................................................................109

Zucchini Cream Cheese Soup ..............................................109

Dinner ..................................................................................110

Cheesy Cauli-Balls with Arugula, Parmesan and Lemon Dressing ...........110

Day 22 ...................................................................................111

Breakfast .............................................................................111

Ricotta Cheese and Berries on Keto Bagels .........................111

Lunch ...................................................................................113

Spinach and Feta Tart .........................................................113

Dinner ..................................................................................115

Zoodle Ramen with Butter Broth ........................................115

Day 23..........................................................................................................117

   Breakfast..................................................................................................117

     Sweet Potato, Egg and Spinach Hash..........................................117

   Lunch.......................................................................................................119

     Brussels Sprouts with Spicy Dressing and Toasted Almonds........119

   Dinner.....................................................................................................120

     Jazzed-up Carbonara (using cauliflower, mushrooms and 3 cheeses)........120

Day 24..........................................................................................................121

   Breakfast..................................................................................................121

     Green smoothie..............................................................................121

   Lunch.......................................................................................................122

     Keto Tabbouleh with Avocado and Yogurt.................................122

   Dinner.....................................................................................................124

     Keto Chili with Sour Cream and Guacamole...............................124

Day 25..........................................................................................................126

   Breakfast..................................................................................................126

     Fat-bomb Iced Coffee....................................................................126

   Lunch.......................................................................................................127

     Egg and Mayo Lettuce Wraps......................................................127

   Dinner.....................................................................................................128

     Fried Rice (cauliflower and broccoli rice) with Eggs and Edamame........128

Day 26..........................................................................................................129

   Breakfast..................................................................................................129

     Vanilla Balls..................................................................................129

   Lunch.......................................................................................................130

     Silken Tofu with Roasted Broccoli and Tangy Dressing.............130

   Dinner.....................................................................................................132

     Veggie Fritters with Fresh Mozzarella........................................132

Day 27..........................................................................................................133

   Breakfast..................................................................................................133

     Overnight Chia Chocolate Pudding.............................................133

   Lunch.......................................................................................................134

     Hasselback Pumpkin.....................................................................134

Dinner ........................................................................................ 136

    Mushroom Puttanesca with Parmesan and Crème Fraiche ................ 136

Day 28 ........................................................................................ 137

  Breakfast ................................................................................... 137

    Cranberry, Yogurt and Almond Milk Smoothie ........................... 137

  Lunch ........................................................................................ 138

    Poached Eggs with Pea, Spinach and Cream Cheese Mash ............ 138

  Dinner ....................................................................................... 140

    Fried Kale Parcels ...................................................................... 140

Day 29 ........................................................................................ 141

  Breakfast ................................................................................... 141

    Blueberry Muffins ...................................................................... 141

  Lunch ........................................................................................ 142

    Eggplant Fries with Garlic Mayonnaise ...................................... 142

  Dinner ....................................................................................... 143

    Fresh Herb, Mozzarella and Roasted Veggie Salad ...................... 143

Day 30 ........................................................................................ 145

  Breakfast ................................................................................... 145

    Yoghurt, Berry and Cream Whip ................................................ 145

  Lunch ........................................................................................ 146

    Broccoli, Leek and Cheddar Soup .............................................. 146

  Dinner ....................................................................................... 147

    Baked Brie with Kale Chips ....................................................... 147

Conclusion .................................................................................. 149

# Introduction

Hello and welcome!

So, let's get straight to it. We are both o n the ketogenic vegetarian journey. It's not easy. So many ketogenic meals include meat, so our options are rather limited. However, I am here to help you to stick to your diet plan while still enjoying some fantastic, tasty meals.

This is *my* take on the ketogenic vegetarian diet. It may be different to yours, but hopefully you'll love it! I have ensured that each and every recipe falls within, or close to, the ketogenic macronutrient guidelines.

Some recipes are a little higher in carbs, but that's okay, as they are paired with lower-carb meals to balance the macros out across the day.

These recipes are packed with vegetables, healthy fats, proteins and lots and lots of flavor. A hint, if you like red chili peppers and fresh herbs, you'll love what's in store for you!

Each recipe has the nutritional information provided (calories, fat, carbs and protein) so you can be sure of what you are putting into your body.

As always, I welcome you to adjust, modify or completely pull apart these recipes to suit your very own tastes. Just make sure they fit with the ketogenic rules. A diet app such as MyFitnessPal comes in handy here!

# What is the ketogenic diet?

The ketogenic diet has a vast and interesting background. I'll give you a really short version so you get the general idea without too much reading!

The Ketogenic diet is a very low-carb, high-fat diet which was popularized by doctors in the 1920s as a way to help people with epilepsy. Ever since, it has remained a relatively common choice of diet and has grown in popularity in recent years. Many people adopt the ketogenic diet for weight loss, but there are many other reasons to try this rather restrictive diet. Increased energy, healthy cholesterol levels, reduced risk of disease, reduced risk of type 2 diabetes...these are a few benefits among many, but we will get deeper into them in more detail soon!

But why is it called "ketogenic"? Because, the desired result of the ketogenic diet is to reach a metabolic state called "ketosis". This is when your body gets the message that there are no carbohydrates being provided, so it must kick into action and find another energy source. So, what does the body do? It uses stored fats! Yup, that stored fat in your body is accessed and used as fuel. But that's not all. Once fat starts to be used as energy (as opposed to carbohydrates and stored glycogen), ketone bodies are produced and used as energy too. Your liver gets the signal to create ketone bodies when the body is deprived of glycogen (this is what carbs are stored as when they enter your system). So, when you have reached "ketosis", all it means is that your body is now using fat and ketones for energy, as opposed to glycogen supplied by carbs.

What does it "look like" to be on the ketogenic diet? Well, the person in question would cut out almost all foods high in carbohydrates and sugars. This includes all starchy and sugary treats such as bread, pasta, rice, baked goods, sweets...you get the picture. What's left is a diet full of non-starchy, low-carb veggies, full-fat dairy (if tolerated), proteins such as eggs and meat (unless you're following a vegetarian diet too!), and small amounts of nuts, seeds, and certain fruits.

## What does it mean to be vegetarian?

This is a question with many answers, depending on the individual person.

Some people choose to live a vegetarian lifestyle for ethical reasons. They believe that the exploitation of animals for the benefit of humans is wrong. Some people disagree with the methods of slaughter and the disregard for the lives of living creatures. Others take an environmental approach to vegetarianism and refuse to support industries which threaten the environment (for example, effluent run-off from cattle, which ruins waterways).

Others do not like to eat meat as the taste, texture and idea of eating another creature just doesn't sit well with them.

And finally, many people cut out meat completely (or heavily reduce it) for health reasons. It has been a contentious topic, whether or not meat (particularly red meat) is harmful or healthy. Studies concerning carcinogens, high cholesterol and heart disease have made many people think about how much meat they consume compared to the amount of fresh fruits and veggies. I won't go into detail about the health risks or benefits of meat, as that's not what this book is about! It's about eating a fresh and healthy keto-vegetarian diet!

Each and every reason for being a vegetarian is completely valid, as it all comes down to personal choice and the freedom to eat and live the way we like.

## Benefits of being on both the ketogenic diet and being a vegetarian

I'll be completely honest. Being on a ketogenic *and* vegetarian diet is rather tricky, as it does wipe out a huge amount of food options. But that's not to say you cannot eat an absolutely *delicious* and satisfying diet every day. What's more, there are so many benefits to this way of eating, you may never want to go back to your old diet.

Here are some of the key benefits of the keto-vegetarian diet.

### Weight loss

Ketosis forces the body to use stored fat for energy, which means your body will become leaner and trimmer. What's more, the ketogenic diet is generally low in calories, which is also a key to weight loss. If you have lots of excess weight to lose, this is awesome news. Your organs will be healthier, your bones will be under less pressure, and you will be more able to exercise more vigorously! If you don't have much, or any weight to lose, you will still enjoy the benefits of a lighter, leaner body with less fat around your organs.

### More energy

People who follow the ketogenic diet find that they have much more energy than they used to. By not giving your body regular doses of carbs and sugars, your blood sugar will be stable and therefore, you won't experience those tiring highs and lows. You might find that you no longer feel sluggish and slow in the afternoon, and that you have a clearer, more alert mind.

### Reduced risk of disease

The risk of developing diabetes, obesity, heart disease and metabolic disease can be reduced by following a ketogenic diet. Lots of veggies and good fats, zero processed sugar and minimal carbs give the body a great chance at remaining healthy into old age. Cutting out all that fried, sugary and starchy food helps the heart to stay clear and strong and the organs to be free of dangerous fat.

### Save money

When you're not allowed to fill your supermarket trolley with alcohol, candy, chocolates, cookies, pasta, bread and all those other tempting things, you end up saving money! What's more, the vegetarian ketogenic diet cuts out the need to buy meat, which can be very expensive! You end up making do with what you have at home, (as long as it's ketogenic), instead of going to the supermarket to stock up on excess foods.

### It could ease gut issues

Many people find that sugar and grains really irritate their gut and wreak havoc on their digestion. By cutting out these culprits and replacing them with more veggies and good fats, many keto-followers find that they experience less bloating and less digestive pain.

# Foods allowed and not allowed on the ketogenic vegetarian diet

Because the goal of the ketogenic diet is to reach ketosis, you really have to follow "the rules" of the ketogenic diet. If you eat too many carbs (or even too many proteins) you will take yourself further and further away from reaching ketosis. So, that brings us to the NO's and the YES's of the ketogenic vegetarian diet!

Here's what you *can eat:*

### *Allowed*

*Leafy, low-carb veggies (including nightshades):*

- Spinach
- Zucchini
- Swiss chard
- Scallions
- Lettuce
- Radish
- Pumpkin
- Tomatoes
- Bell peppers
- Onions (not too much, but enough to flavor your meals)
- Kale
- Bok choy
- Pak choy
- Cucumber
- Eggplant
- Celery
- Cauliflower
- Asparagus
- Brussels Sprouts
- Carrots (in small doses)
- Broccoli

*Green beans: if you're desperate for green beans, you can enjoy small portions of them*

*Fruits: some, not all*

- Avocado
- Lemons
- Limes

*A small portion of berries: raspberries, strawberries, blackberries, blueberries, just use them sparingly*

*Herbs and spices for flavor:*

You can use as many herbs and spices as you like, as long as they are not combined with other ingredients (i.e. rubs and marinades). Just use plain spices and fresh or dried herbs.

Here are some of my favorite dried spices to use on the Ketogenic diet:

- Cumin
- Paprika
- Chili powder
- Garam masala
- Powdered ginger
- Dried and ground coriander (cilantro)
- Cinnamon
- Black pepper

And here are my favorite fresh herbs:

- Cilantro
- Parsley
- Thyme
- Rosemary
- Dill
- Oregano
- Basil

Those are just a few of my favorites. If you have lots of fabulous fresh herbs and dried spices in your garden or pantry, throw them into your meals! They will create rich, vibrant and tasty flavors.

*Fats:*

- Butter
- Ghee (clarified butter which is made by melting butter, skimming the foam off the top, and draining through a strainer to remove milk solids)
- Coconut oil
- Avocado oil
- Olive oil
- Flaxseed oil

*Nuts/seeds:*

Yes, you can have a small portion of nuts and seeds to add crunch, flavor and substance to your meals. However, don't overdo it, as you can easily have too much and end up going way over your carb-count. I like to toast a few nuts or seeds to add to salads.

- Chia seeds
- Linseeds/flaxseeds
- Almonds (almond butter is good too)
- Macadamia nuts
- Sunflower seeds
- Pumpkin seeds
- Sesame seeds
- Pecan nuts
- Pistachio nuts
- Hazelnuts
- Pine nuts

Sorry, no peanuts allowed on keto (I mean, you could have one or two, but that's just going to be too tempting!). Peanuts are in the same family as beans and chickpeas etc. so they're out of bounds.

*Dairy and eggs:*

- Eggs
- Full-fat Greek yogurt
- Cream (heavy, full-fat)
- Cheeses (Parmesan and cheddar are great as they're full of flavor so you don't need as much)

*Drinks:*

- Coffee, black or with cream
- Tea (green, herbal, black)
- Nut milks (make sure they have NO added sugar) and use in moderation
- Sparkling water

Water flavored with lemon slices is an ideal drink on the ketogenic diet

It's best to avoid alcohol, but clear spirits such as vodka or gin with no mixers are the best ones to choose. Stay well away from wine, beer, cocktails and pre-mixed drinks.

## Not Allowed

*Starchy veggies:*

- Potatoes
- Peas

NOTE: you can have a small amount of carrot and sweet potato. Think of it as a flavor, not as the main basis of the dish.

*Fruits:*

Basically, all fruits except berries and citrus should be avoided. Even with citrus, just enjoy a little squeeze of lemon, orange or lime juice, but avoid eating the whole fruit. Always avoid bananas as they are a high-carb fruit.

*Soft drinks:*

- No sugary sodas allowed!
- No fruit juices allowed (stick to water, coffee with cream, herbal tea)

*Bread:*

NO bread allowed unless it has been made with keto-friendly ingredients. I find it easier to avoid bread all together

*Rice:*

- No rice of any kind is allowed

*Pasta:*

- Absolutely none

*Flours:*

- Plain flours are not allowed
- Almond and coconut flour are allowed in small doses

*Grains:*

- No oats, barley, rye, corn, quinoa, cereal etc.
- If it's grainy and starchy? It's not allowed

*Legumes and pulses:*

- No beans of any kind are allowed
- No chickpeas
- No lentils

*Sugar:*

- NONE allowed!

*Cakes and baked goods*:

- Unless it has been made especially for the keto diet, no baked goods are allowed. No cookies, cakes, bars, pies, tarts… it's all off limits

*Treats:*

- Ice cream, candy, anything you already know as strictly a "treat food" is not allowed!

Except...a very, very small portion of dark chocolate with a high cocoa percentage

# 30-day meal plan

## About these recipes

I have aimed for an overall intake of 30 - 50 grams of carbohydrates a day, spread across breakfast, lunch and dinner. Depending on your weight, height and desired calorie-intake, this might need to be very slightly adjusted. If you do need to eat less carbohydrates than what these recipes provide, simply reduce the amount of the higher-carb foods in the recipe.

I would say that these recipes are on the higher-carb scale of the ketogenic diet, which might not sit well with some people. That's okay! You can simply halve the ingredients with the highest carb-count.

On some days, the most carb-heavy meals tend to be dinner. This might seem odd to people who follow the no-carbs-at-night idea. However, I personally find that I like to have a little more substance with my dinner at night. In the morning, I don't want a heavy breakfast so I prefer a fat and protein-rich meal. By the time I get to sit down to my plate of deliciousness at night, I want something to fill and satisfy me! And for me, the foods to do the job are...ironically, more carb-heavy. This doesn't mean that my keto plans are dashed, as long as I stay within my macro parameters.

Because the keto-vegetarian diet is restrictive in nature, you may find that there are a few ingredients which are repeated regularly throughout these recipes. Hopefully you won't tire of them too quickly!

Some recipes cater to 1 person, some cater to 2, and some cater to 4. Many of the breakfast recipes cater to 1 or 2 people, as I find that I don't often make breakfast for anyone else but me, but sometimes I will add another serving to the mix for my partner. Whereas dinner time is usually the time when we serve our family or a group of friends, so many of the dinner recipes cater to 4 people.

# Day 1

## Breakfast

### *Cauliflower Cakes*

*I adore these cauliflower cakes because they are light yet satisfying, tasty and fresh. You can serve them with a poached egg or two, but make sure you count the extra macros to make sure you're still within keto parameters.*

Servings: 4

Time: approximately 25 minutes

**Nutritional info:**

- Calories: 180
- Fat: 7.3 grams
- Carbs: 5.8 grams
- Protein: 7.5 grams

**Ingredients:**

- 4 cups cauliflower, (small pieces)
- 1 cup grated cheddar cheese
- 2 eggs, lightly beaten
- 1 tsp. paprika
- 1 tsp. chili powder
- Salt and pepper
- ½ cup fresh parsley, finely chopped
- 1 Tbsp. olive oil

**Directions:**

1. Place the cauliflower, cheese, eggs, paprika, chili, salt, pepper and parsley into a large bowl and stir to combine.
2. Drizzle the olive oil into a frying pan and place over a medium-high heat.
3. While the pan heats, shape the cauliflower mixture into 12 even patties.
4. Once the oil is hot, fry the cakes on both sides until golden.
5. Serve hot or warm, with an extra drizzle of olive oil and a poached egg if you desire!

# Lunch

## *Leafy Green Salad with Olives, Cheese and Almonds*

*Because we are having pretty substantial meals for breakfast and dinner, a fresh, light salad for lunch is the best option. However, the feta cheese, olives and almonds provide texture, flavor and a satisfying saltiness.*

Servings: 4

Time: approximately 10 minutes (no cooking required!)

## Nutritional info:

- Calories: 202
- Fat: 16 grams
- Carbs: 8.1 grams
- Protein: 8 grams

## Ingredients:

- 6 cups shredded lettuce (cos or romaine)
- 4 cups baby spinach (fresh, raw)
- 8 black olives, pits removed, sliced into small pieces
- 3 oz. feta cheese, crumbled into small pieces
- ¼ cup raw almonds, roughly chopped
- 2 Tbsp. olive oil
- Juice of 1 lemon
- Salt and pepper

## Directions:

1. Place the lettuce, spinach, olives, feta and almonds into a large bowl, toss to combine.
2. Place the olive oil, lemon juice, salt and pepper into a small glass and stir to thoroughly combine to make a light dressing.
3. Pour the dressing over the salad before serving and lightly toss.

# Dinner

## *Roasted Pumpkin and Cilantro Side Salad*

*Pumpkin is frowned-upon in large quantities on the ketogenic diet. However, a small amount as part of your dinner or lunch is perfectly fine if the macros match up. I find pumpkin to be a satisfying and filling food to eat whilst on the keto diet, as it reminds me of potatoes! Creamy mozzarella adds extra fat, protein and flavor.*

Servings: 4

Time: approximately 30 minutes

### Nutritional info:

- Calories: 160
- Fat: 11.4 grams
- Carbs: 9.8 grams
- Protein: 6.2 grams

### Ingredients:

- 3 cups cubed pumpkin
- 2 Tbsp. olive oil
- ½ red onion, finely chopped
- ¼ cup fresh cilantro, roughly chopped
- 1 red chili pepper, finely chopped
- 3.5 oz. fresh mozzarella cheese, broken into small pieces
- Salt and pepper to season

### Directions:

1. Preheat your oven to 375 degrees Fahrenheit and line a baking tray with baking paper.
2. Place the cubed pumpkin onto the tray, drizzle over half of the olive oil (1 Tbsp.) and sprinkle salt and pepper over top.
3. Bake for approximately 25 minutes or until soft and golden.
4. Place the cooked pumpkin into a serving bowl.
5. Add the remaining olive oil, red onion, cilantro, chili, mozzarella, salt and pepper.
6. Stir to combine.
7. Serve warm or cold, it's great either way.

# Day 2

## Breakfast

### *Eggs and Avocado with Spicy Olive Oil Drizzle*

*This breakfast is full of good fats and proteins to keep you full until lunchtime. The spicy olive oil can be used with any dish you like! I find that it adds a special kick to the meal.*

Servings: 2

Time: approximately 12 minutes

**Nutritional info:**

- Calories: 385
- Fat: 33.5 grams
- Carbs: 8 grams
- Protein: 14.3 grams

**Ingredients:**

- 4 eggs
- 1 large avocado, cut into quarters, (skin and stone discarded)
- Salt and pepper
- 2 Tbsp. olive oil
- 1 tsp. garlic powder
- ¼ fresh red chili, finely chopped

**Directions:**

1. Bring a pot of shallow water to the boil.
2. Carefully crack the eggs into the water and leave to poach for a couple of minutes until they reach your desired doneness, I like my yolks to be as runny as possible.
3. Use a slotted spoon to fish the eggs out of the water, and place two on a plate.
4. Place avocado slices onto the plates next to the eggs.
5. Sprinkle the eggs and avocado with salt and pepper.

6. Place the olive oil, garlic powder and chili into a small cup and stir vigorously to combine.
7. Drizzle the oil over the eggs and avocado just before serving.
8. If you are serving a non-keto friend, just throw a piece or two of toast on their plate and they'll be happy!

# Lunch

## *Asparagus Tart*

*This tart doesn't have any pastry or crust. Instead, the asparagus sits on a soft base of egg, with cheese sprinkled over the top. This can also be enjoyed for breakfast or dinner!*

Servings: 4

Time: approximately 25 minutes

## Nutritional info:

- Calories: 160
- Fat: 10.5 grams
- Carbs: 5.4 grams
- Protein: 12.1 grams

## Ingredients:

- 4 eggs
- 1 garlic clove, minced or very finely chopped
- Salt and pepper
- 20 asparagus spears, woody ends removed
- ½ cup grated cheddar cheese
- 2 Tbsp. chopped walnuts

## Directions:

1. Preheat your oven to 375 degrees Fahrenheit and grease a pie dish with butter or oil spray.
2. Place the eggs, garlic, salt and pepper into a small bowl and beat with a fork.
3. Pour the eggs into the tray.
4. Lay the asparagus onto the eggs in one tidy row.
5. Sprinkle the grated cheese over the asparagus.
6. Place into the oven and cook for approximately 12 minutes or until the cheese has melted, the eggs are set, and the asparagus is just cooked but still a little crunchy.

# Dinner

## *Spinach and Leek No-crust Quiche*

*This quiche is light, cheesy, fresh and very filling. The baking powder gives it a "lift" while the spinach adds that crucial green goodness. It is quite high in protein, so don't go overboard with your serving sizes. Serve it with a fresh salad of tomatoes, lettuce and cucumber for extra nutritional value.*

Servings: 4

Time: approximately 25 minutes

### Nutritional info:

- Calories: 297
- Fat: 14.3 grams
- Carbs: 9 grams
- Protein: 16.4 grams

### Ingredients:

- 1 Tbsp. olive oil
- 4 cups spinach, finely chopped
- 2 medium-sized leeks, finely sliced
- 8 eggs, lightly beaten
- 1 cup grated cheddar cheese
- 1 tsp. baking powder
- Salt and pepper

### Directions:

1. Preheat your oven to 320 degrees Fahrenheit and grease a baking dish with butter or oil spray.
2. Drizzle the olive oil into a frying pan over a medium heat.
3. Once the oil is nice and hot, add the spinach and leeks, sauté for a few minutes until the spinach has wilted and the leeks are transparent.

4. Place the cooked spinach and leeks into a large bowl and add the eggs, cheddar, baking powder, salt and pepper.
5. Stir to thoroughly combine.
6. Pour the mixture into your greased baking dish and place into the oven for approximately 15 minutes or until just set and starting to turn golden.
7. Leave to cool slightly and serve warm or cold.
8. A fresh, leafy salad goes really well with this dish!

# Day 3

## Breakfast

### *Baked Eggs with Tomato and Basil*

*Eggs are baked in the oven in a delicious sea of tomato, basil and a hint of chili and garlic. A great keto-friendly breakfast for people who love savory flavors in the morning.*

Servings: 2

Time: approximately 20 minutes

**Nutritional info:**

- Calories: 235
- Fat: 16.4 grams
- Carbs: 7 grams
- Protein: 14.5 grams

**Ingredients:**

- 1 garlic clove, minced or finely chopped
- 1 cup canned tomatoes (the pre-chopped kind!)
- ¼ cup fresh basil leaves, roughly chopped
- ½ tsp. chili powder or chili flakes
- 1 Tbsp. olive oil
- 4 eggs
- Salt and pepper

**Directions:**

1. Preheat the oven to 375 degrees Fahrenheit and grease a small baking dish with olive oil.
2. Place the garlic, tomatoes, basil, chili and olive oil into the dish and stir to combine.
3. Crack the eggs into the dish, leaving space between each egg.

4. Sprinkle the whole dish with salt and pepper.
5. Place into the oven and cook for approximately 12 minutes or until the eggs are set and the tomatoes are gently bubbling.
6. Serve with extra basil sprinkled over top!

# Lunch

## *"Hot Dogs" with Mustard and Cheese*

*Okay, so it's a bit of a stretch to call this a "hot dog", but when we are on a keto/vegetarian diet, we have to get creative! Full of fresh veggies, a hint of cheese and some hot mustard.*

Servings: 4

Time: approximately 20 minutes

## Nutritional info:

- Calories: 230
- Fat: 16.4 grams
- Carbs: 9.6 grams
- Protein: 13.5 grams

## Ingredients:

- 2 cups white button mushrooms
- 1 cup raw cauliflower pieces
- 1 cup pumpkin cubes, steamed or microwaved until soft
- 2 eggs
- ¼ cup grated cheddar cheese
- Salt and pepper
- Olive oil for frying
- 1 tsp. wholegrain mustard per serving

## Directions:

1. Place the mushrooms and cauliflower into a food processor and blitz until the pieces are small and starting to stick together.
2. Add the cooked pumpkin, eggs, cheese, salt and pepper to the food processor and blitz until it comes together to form a thick batter.
3. Drizzle the olive oil into a frying pan and place over a medium heat.

4. While the pan is heating up, roll the hot dog mixture into long logs, or even patties if you prefer or find it easier.
5. Fry the dogs or patties on both sides until golden.
6. Serve with a dash of hot mustard and a fresh green salad on the side if you wish!

# Dinner

## *Broccoli, Almond and Feta Salad*

*This is an incredibly easy salad to prepare, and it's extremely tasty too. It is slightly higher on the carb scale, but that's okay. Just ensure that your snack choices are zero-carb today! It's light and not exactly "comfort food", which is perfect for days when you're not ravenous, but you do need a little something to enjoy for dinner.*

Servings: 4

Time: approximately 20 minutes

### Nutritional info:

- Calories: 190
- Fat: 13.5 grams
- Carbs: 11.8 grams
- Protein: 8.2 grams

### Ingredients:

- 1 large head of broccoli, cut into florets (remove the core first)
- ¼ cup slivered almonds
- 2 oz. feta cheese, crumbled
- 2 Tbsp. olive oil
- Salt and pepper
- Juice of ½ lemon

### Directions:

1. Steam the broccoli either in the microwave or by using a double boiler. Don't overcook! You want it to retain some crispiness.
2. Place the cooked broccoli into a large serving bowl and add the slivered almonds, feta cheese, olive oil, salt, pepper and lemon juice.
3. Stir to thoroughly combine.
4. Serve warm or cold.

# Day 4

## Breakfast

### *Brussels Sprout and Zucchini Hash*

*This recipe has a little more carbs than others, due to the Brussels sprouts. However, we are having a carb-light dinner so it all balances out! If you hate Brussels sprouts, I urge you to give this recipe a try, they are so nutritious and actually very tasty when cooked with cheese, onion and other tasty ingredients! I think you'll love it.*

Servings: 4

Time: approximately 20 minutes

**Nutritional information:**

- Calories: 290
- Fat: 14.5 grams
- Carbs: 14 grams
- Protein: 11 grams

**Ingredients:**

- 2 Tbsp. olive oil
- 3 medium zucchinis, sliced
- 1 large onion, finely chopped
- 10 Brussels sprouts, roughly chopped
- ¼ cup almond meal
- 2 eggs, lightly beaten
- 1 cup grated cheddar cheese
- Salt and pepper

**Directions:**

1. Drizzle the olive oil into a frying pan and place over a medium heat.
2. Once the oil is hot, add the zucchini, onion, Brussels sprouts and almond meal, stir as the veggies cook and soften, about 5-7 minutes.

3. Once the veggies are soft and golden, crack the eggs into the pan and stir to break them up.
4. Leave for about a minute to allow the eggs to gently cook.
5. Sprinkle the cheese over the dish and gently stir through, leave for about a minute until the cheese melts.
6. Sprinkle with salt and pepper before serving.

# Lunch

## *Sesame Seed Sushi (Cucumber, Quinoa, Carrot, Mayo and Sesame Seeds)*

*This sushi has a little, tiny bit of quinoa to bulk it out and provide protein. Veggies, sesame seeds and creamy mayo come together to make a fresh and moreish lunch. Remember to thoroughly rinse your quinoa before cooking to remove the bitter coating.*

Servings: 2

Time: approximately 20 minutes

## Nutritional info:

- Calories: 200
- Fat: 13 grams
- Carbs: 15.4 grams
- Protein: 5 grams

## Ingredients:

- 1/3 cup cooked quinoa (follow the packet instructions to cook)
- 4 nori sheets (roasted seaweed)
- ½ cucumber, cut into strips lengthways
- ½ carrot, cut into thin strips, lengthways
- 2 Tbsp. full-fat egg mayonnaise
- 1 Tbsp. sesame seeds, gently toasted on a dry pan

## Directions:

1. Prepare the quinoa according to the packet instructions, (rinse and drain it first!).
2. Lay the nori sheets out onto a clean board.
3. Spread a thin layer of cooked quinoa over each nori sheet.
4. Layer the cucumber and carrot into a pile in the middle of the nori sheet, along the width.
5. Spread or dollop the mayonnaise over the veggies.
6. sprinkle the sesame seeds over the mayonnaise.
7. Roll the filled nori sheets tightly and seal the ends with warm water.
8. Slice and eat!

# Dinner

## *Sautéed Spinach and Kale with Halloumi and Fresh Chili*

*This is a dinner with strong, salty flavors thanks to the halloumi. If you've never tried halloumi, you're in for such a treat! It is a hard, creamy, salty cheese which gets golden and crispy when fried.*

Serving: 4

Time: approximately 25 minutes

### Nutritional info:

- Calories: 156
- Fat: 11 grams
- Carbs: 7.2 grams
- Protein: 8.3 grams

### Ingredients:

- 1 Tbsp. olive oil
- 4 cups baby spinach
- 1 cup kale, finely chopped, (tough stalks removed)
- 4 oz. halloumi cheese, sliced
- 1 fresh red chili, finely chopped
- ¼ cup chopped fresh parsley
- Juice of ½ lemon
- Salt and pepper

### Directions:

1. Drizzle the olive oil into a frying pan and place over a medium heat.
2. Once the oil is hot, add the spinach and kale and a pinch of salt and pepper.
3. Sauté for a few minutes, until wilted.
4. Add the chili and stir through.
5. Push the spinach and kale to one side of the frying pan to make room for the haloumi.

6. Place the halloumi slices onto the hot pan and fry on both sides until golden and crispy.
7. Serve the halloumi on top of a pile of spinach and kale, with a squeeze of lemon juice and a sprinkle of salt and pepper.

# Day 5

## Breakfast

### *Green Smoothie*

*A good old green smoothie gets the day started right. Because yesterday was a little more carb-heavy, we are starting today with a really low-carb breakfast to make sure everything is nice and balanced! Tasty, hydrating and full of nutrients. This recipe makes enough for one large smoothie, so just double the ingredients if you are sharing with a buddy.*

Servings: 1

Time: 5 minutes

## Nutritional info:
- Calories: 305
- Fat: 28.6 grams
- Carbs: 11 grams
- Protein: 7 grams

## Ingredients:
- 2 cups baby spinach leaves
- ¼ cup strawberries, chopped (you can use frozen if you like)
- ½ cup full-fat coconut cream
- ½ cup ice
- ½ cup chopped cucumber
- 1 Tbsp. olive oil, coconut oil or flaxseed oil
- Optional: liquid stevia to add sweetness if you prefer a sweeter smoothie

## Directions:
1. Place all ingredients into a blender, blitz until smooth.
2. Pour into your smoothie glass or takeaway cup and enjoy!

# Lunch

## *Cheese and Tomato Toasties (with Eggplant Bread)*

*Depending on where in the world you live, you might be wondering what a "toastie" is! Well, it's basically like a grilled cheese sandwich, which is referred to as a "toasted sandwich" or "toastie" in some countries. Instead of bread, we have eggplant. And the filling? Tomato and cheese!*

Servings: 2

Time: approximately 30 minutes

### Nutritional info:

- Calories: 340
- Fat: 24 grams
- Carbs: 18.3 grams
- Protein: 12.5 grams

### Ingredients:

- 1 large eggplant, cut into 4 slices lengthways
- 2 Tbsp. olive oil
- 1 large tomato, sliced
- 4 oz. mozzarella cheese, sliced
- Salt and pepper

### Directions:

1. Brush the eggplant slices with olive oil.
2. Place a frying pan or skillet over a medium heat.
3. Once the pan is hot, place 2 eggplant slices onto the pan.
4. Place 2 slices of tomato and 2 slices of mozzarella onto the eggplant and sprinkle with salt and pepper.
5. Place another eggplant slice on top.
6. Leave to grill for about 2 minutes before carefully flipping the sandwich over and grilling the other side.
7. When both sides are golden and the cheese has melted, the sandwiches are ready to eat!

# Dinner

## *Tofu and Asparagus Stir Fry*

*This is a very light dinner with very little carbohydrates and lots of good fats and proteins. If asparagus isn't your thing, or you find it hard to source, swap it out for another green veggie such as broccoli.*

Servings: 4

Time: approximately 45 minutes

### Nutritional info:

- Calories: 180
- Fat: 17.5 grams
- Carbs: 6 grams
- Protein: 17.6 grams

### Ingredients:

- 1 Tbsp. olive oil
- 9 oz. firm tofu, cut into cubes
- 12 asparagus spears, woody ends cut off, cut into small pieces
- 2 garlic cloves, minced or finely chopped
- 1 cup spinach, roughly chopped
- 1 Tbsp. soy sauce (low carb)
- Fresh cilantro, roughly chopped
- A pinch of fresh red chili if you like a bit of heat

### Directions:

1. Heat a wok or frying pan over a high heat.
2. Drizzle the olive oil into the pan and leave to heat for a few seconds.
3. Add the tofu and stir as it fries.
4. Once the tofu is golden, add the asparagus and stir as the asparagus pieces cook, about 2 minutes, you still want the asparagus to be crunchy.
5. Add the garlic and spinach and stir while the spinach wilts.
6. Add the soy sauce, cilantro and chili if using, give a quick stir to combine.
7. Serve immediately!

# Day 6

## Breakfast

### *Swiss Chard Omelet*

*Eggs and green veggies, what's a better keto breakfast than that? With a pinch of garlic salt and a good knob of butter, this omelet is tasty enough to take you from breakfast to lunch without cravings in between.*

Servings: 2

Time: approximately 12 minutes

## Nutritional info:

- Calories: 260
- Fat: 21.2 grams
- Carbs: 3.4 grams
- Protein: 14 grams

## Ingredients:

- 4 eggs, lightly beaten
- 4 cups Swiss chard, sliced
- 2 Tbsp. butter
- ½ tsp. garlic salt
- Fresh pepper

## Directions:

1. Place the butter into a non-stick frying pan and place over a low-medium heat.
2. Once the butter has melted, add the Swiss chard and stir as it cooks and wilts, about 2 minutes.
3. Pour the eggs into the pan and gently stir them into the Swiss chard.
4. Sprinkle garlic salt and pepper over the top.
5. Leave the omelet to gently cook for about 2 minutes or until just set.
6. Serve immediately!

# Lunch

## *Leek and Feta Salad with Pistachios*

*This salad has a real kick of saltiness and texture, provided by the feta and pistachios. The onion-like flavor of leeks is warming, satisfying and very tasty. Because our breakfast was very light on carbs, we can afford to have a little more with lunch.*

Servings: 2

Time: approximately 20 minutes

## Nutritional info:

- Calories: 310
- Fat: 28 grams
- Carbs: 23 grams
- Protein: 14 grams

## Ingredients:

- 2 Tbsp. butter
- 2 medium leeks, washed and sliced
- 4 cups shredded iceberg lettuce
- 3.5 oz. feta cheese, cut into small pieces
- ¼ cup pistachio nuts (shelled)
- Salt and pepper
- Fresh parsley, finely chopped

## Directions:

1. Place the butter into a frying pan and place over a medium heat.
2. Once the butter has melted, add the leeks to the pan and stir as they become soft and translucent, set aside to slightly cool.
3. Place the lettuce, feta, pistachio nuts, salt, pepper and parsley into a large bowl, toss to combine.

4. Add the leeks to the bowl and gently toss to incorporate them into the salad.
5. I find that the "butteriness" of the leeks is enough to double as a very light dressing, so I don't add anything extra at the end. You could squeeze some fresh lemon juice or balsamic vinegar over the top if you wish.

# Dinner

## *Roasted Zucchini with Garlic Butter and Cauliflower Rice*

*This might come across as a very odd combination. However, I stumbled across it one night when I only had a few measly ingredients to work with, so I threw them together. Zucchini becomes deliciously soft and gooey when roasted, and the garlic butter...well, I could drink it!*

*Cauliflower rice bulks the meal out without adding banned carbs.*

*This is a really light dinner with hardly any calories, which means you can and should add more keto-friendly snacks during the day. Greek yogurt is ideal, as is celery with nut butter.*

Serving: 4

Time: approximately 25 minutes

## Nutritional info:

- Calories: 150
- Fat: 12 grams
- Carbs: 9 grams
- Protein: 2.5 grams

## Ingredients:

- 3 zucchini, cut into slices
- 1 Tbsp. olive oil
- 3 cups raw cauliflower, blitzed in a food processor until the size of rice
- 3 Tbsp. butter
- 3 garlic cloves, minced or very finely chopped
- ½ tsp. chili powder
- Salt and pepper

## Directions:

1. Preheat the oven to 375 degrees Fahrenheit and line a baking tray with baking paper.

2. Place the zucchini slices onto the tray, drizzle with the olive oil, and sprinkle with salt and pepper.
3. Roast the zucchinis for approximately 15-20 minutes or until golden and soft.
4. Place the cauliflower rice into a microwave-safe bowl and cook in the microwave for 2 minutes, stirring once (at the 1-minute mark).
5. Place the butter into a small pot or saucepan and add the garlic, place over a low heat and stir as the butter melts, set aside to cool slightly.
6. Place the cooked zucchini over a bed of cauliflower rice, drizzle some garlic butter over the top, then sprinkle with chili powder, salt and pepper.

# Day 7

## Breakfast

### *Greek Yogurt and Berry Parfait*

*Berries are generally an occasional food on the Keto diet, as they can be high in carbs and sugars. However, they are also high in vitamins and other great nutrients...plus they are delicious. Go ahead and enjoy this gorgeous berry and yogurt parfait without any reservations!*

Servings: 1

Time: approximately 10 minutes

### Nutritional info:

- Calories: 380
- Fat: 25.5 grams
- Carbs: 15.8 grams
- Protein: 23.3 grams

### Ingredients:

- 1 cup full-fat Greek yogurt, (plain, unsweetened, no flavors added)
- 1 Tbsp. pumpkin seeds
- 1/3 cup mixed fresh or frozen berries, (if using frozen, leave to thaw)
- 2 tsp. flaxseed oil
- Pinch of cinnamon

### Directions:

1. Find a glass cup, sundae dish, or small bowl.
2. Place half of the yogurt into the dish.
3. Sprinkle over a few of the pumpkin seeds.
4. Add half of the berries to the dish.
5. Drizzle over half of the flaxseed oil.
6. Layer the rest of the yoghurt, seeds, berries, and flaxseed oil into the dish.
7. Sprinkle the top with a little pinch of cinnamon for flavor and prettiness.

# Lunch

## *Olive, Red Onion, Cheese and Spinach Salad*

*A quick salad with strong flavors and zero cooking required. If you want to avoid onion breath...keep the onions out. If you hate olives? Leave those out too...in fact, this might be a salad for specific tastes! Hopefully it suits your palate.*

Servings: 2

Time: approximately 10 minutes

### Nutritional info:

- Calories: 285
- Fat: 25 grams
- Carbs: 7 grams
- Protein: 7.8 grams

### Ingredients:

- 4 cups baby spinach leaves
- ½ red onion, finely chopped
- 6 black olives, pitted, roughly chopped
- ½ cucumber, cut into chunks
- 2 oz. cheese (use your favorite, or what you have on hand) cut into small cubes
- 2 Tbsp. olive oil
- 1 Tbsp. apple cider vinegar
- Salt and pepper

### Directions:

1. Place the spinach, onions, olives, cucumber and cheese into a large bowl and toss to combine.
2. Divide the salad between two bowls or two Tupperware containers.
3. Mix together the olive oil, apple cider vinegar, salt and pepper in a small bowl or cup and drizzle over the two salads before eating or storing in the fridge until lunchtime.

# Dinner

## *Butternut and Garlic Soup*

*Butternut squash makes for such a smooth and creamy soup, and the addition of garlic just makes it that much tastier.*

Serving: 4

Time:  approximately 35 minutes

## Nutritional info:

- Calories: 187
- Fat: 11.3 grams
- Carbs: 20 grams
- Protein: 3 grams

## Ingredients:

- 4 cups butternut squash, cubed (skin and seeds removed)
- 2 garlic cloves, finely chopped
- 4 cups vegetable broth (stock)
- Salt and pepper
- ½ cup full-fat cream

## Directions:

1. Place the butternut squash, garlic cloves, broth, salt and pepper into a large pot over a medium heat, cover.
2. Leave the pot to come to the boil, then reduce the temperature so that the soup is gently simmering.
3. Once the squash is very soft, turn off the heat and leave to cool slightly.
4. Use hand-held blender to blitz the soup into a smooth, creamy consistency.
5. Stir the cream through the soup before serving.

# Day 8

## Breakfast

### *Pancakes*

*Yup, pancakes. These are keto pancakes which are made with amazing ingredients such as cream cheese, egg, vanilla and almond flour. Even when I'm not on the keto diet, I still make these all the time as they're so delicious.*

Servings: 4

Time: approximately 30 minutes

## Nutritional info:

- Calories: 180
- Fat: 15.7 grams
- Carbs: 3 grams
- Protein: 7.3 grams

## Ingredients:

- 3 oz. cream cheese (plain, full-fat)
- 3 eggs
- 3 Tbsp. almond flour (ground almonds)
- 2 tsp. vanilla extract
- ½ tsp. baking soda
- Butter for frying
- Stevia or other natural sweetener you like (I don't usually use any sweetener, but you can add a few drops if you want sweeter pancakes, just start with a little bit and add more to taste)

## Directions:

1. Place the cream cheese, eggs, almond flour, vanilla and baking soda into a bowl (add your sweetener now too, if using) and beat with a wooden spoon until smooth.

This might take a little elbow grease to get the cream cheese incorporated with the other ingredients, but give it all you've got.

2. Place a non-stick frying pan over a medium heat and add a small knob of butter.
3. Once the butter has melted, add even dollops of pancake batter into the pan, leaving room for them to spread, about 2 or 3 pancakes per batch.
4. When you see bubbles appearing, flip the pancakes over to cook the other side until golden.
5. Serve and enjoy!

# Lunch

## *Egg and Greens Salad with Yogurt Mint Dressing*

*Another trusty salad for lunch. This one has eggs, broccoli, bell pepper and a little hint of lime and mint to spike the yogurt dressing.*

Servings: 2

Time: approximately 20 minutes

### Nutritional info:

- Calories: 215
- Fat: 10 grams
- Carbs: 13 grams
- Protein: 22 grams

### Ingredients:

- 4 eggs, hard boiled (you know how to do this!)
- 1 small-medium head of broccoli, cut into florets
- 1 green bell pepper, seeds removed, sliced
- 2 cups baby spinach
- 2 cups lettuce, roughly chopped
- Salt and pepper
- ½ cup Greek yogurt
- Juice of 1 lime
- Handful of fresh mint leaves, finely chopped

### Directions:

1. Place the broccoli into a microwave-safe bowl and add a small dash of water (about 2 Tbsp.), cover and cook on high for 1-minute increments until cooked but still crunchy.
2. Cut the hard-boiled eggs into quarters and set aside
3. Place the bell pepper, spinach, lettuce, broccoli, salt and pepper into a salad bowl and toss to combine.

4. Carefully place the eggs on top of the salad (I don't toss them in, as they will break).
5. In a cup or small bowl, mix together the yogurt, lime juice and mint leaves until combined.
6. Drizzle the yogurt dressing over the salad before serving!

# Dinner

## *Cucumber and Tofu Summer Rolls*

*In case we differ in geographical backgrounds, Summer rolls (to me!) are fresh rice paper rolls, filled with veggies and all kinds of delicious things. These Summer rolls are keto-friendly, (and vegetarian) so they have lettuce instead of rice paper wrappers.*

Serving: 4

Time: approximately 25 minutes

### Nutritional info:

- Calories: 160
- Fat: 11.2 grams
- Carbs: 10 grams
- Protein: 6 grams

### Ingredients:

- 4 oz. firm tofu, sliced
- 1 Tbsp. sesame oil
- 2 Tbsp. soy sauce
- 1 fresh iceberg lettuce, dirty or torn outer leaves discarded
- 1 avocado, flesh sliced
- ½ cucumber, sliced
- 1 red bell pepper, seeds removed, sliced
- 1 Tbsp. walnuts

### Directions:

1. Place the tofu, sesame oil and soy sauce into a small bowl and allow the tofu to marinate while you prep the veggies.
2. Once the veggies are prepped, place a frying pan over a medium-high heat, once it is hot, add the tofu and marinade to the pan and fry until the tofu is cooked and golden (about 4 minutes).

3. Remove the tofu from the heat and let it cool slightly.
4. Make your summer rolls by laying lettuce leaves onto a clean board and making a neat pile of tofu, avocado, cucumber, bell pepper and walnuts in the center of the leaf.
5. Tightly roll the Summer rolls before enjoying!

# Day 9

## Breakfast

### *Soft-Boiled Eggs with Asparagus Spears*

*This is a breakfast for when you've got a bit more time on your hands in the morning. I find it is a great way to make sure I'm getting enough protein and good fat to start the day off, as well as those vital greens.*

Serving: 1

Time: approximately 15 minutes

## Nutritional info:

- Calories: 385
- Fat: 34.5 grams
- Carbs: 3.7 grams
- Protein: 14.7 grams

## Ingredients:

- Dash of vinegar
- 2 eggs
- 6 asparagus spears
- 1 tsp. olive oil
- 1 tsp. butter
- Salt and pepper

## Directions:

1. Bring a pot of water to a rapid boil and add a dash of vinegar.
2. Very gently place the eggs into the water with a large spoon.
3. Set a timer for 4 minutes.
4. As soon as the timer beeps, place the pot under a cold running tap until the water surrounding the eggs is cold.

5.  While the eggs are boiling, place a small frying pan over a high heat and add the butter and olive oil.
6.  Once the butter has melted, place the asparagus into the pan and fry until golden and just beginning to soften, turning a couple of times as they cook.
7.  Place the boiled eggs into your egg cup and set the asparagus next to them.
8.  Sprinkle the asparagus with salt and pepper before devouring!
9.  To eat: crack the top off the egg with a spoon and dunk your asparagus into the yolk.

**NOTE:** I know that there are many different ways to boil eggs, (some people use simmering water as opposed to a rapid boil etc.), so if my way doesn't appeal to you, just boil them your way! The result is the same in the end.

# Lunch

## *Roasted Veggies with Cheese Balls (Goat Cheese Coated in Seeds)*

*Roasted veggies with a dash of balsamic vinegar. That's not all! Goats cheese and cream cheese combine to create salty, creamy morsels of goodness, coated in toasted seeds.*

Serving: 2

Time: approximately 30 minutes

## Nutritional info:

- Calories: 410
- Fat: 27.5 grams
- Carbs: 30 grams
- Protein: 16 grams

## Ingredients:

- 1 red bell pepper, seeds removed, sliced
- 1 large zucchini, sliced
- 2 large Portobello mushrooms, sliced
- 1 cup pumpkin, cubed (skin removed)
- 1 small-medium broccoli, cut into florets
- 2 Tbsp. olive oil
- 2 oz. cream cheese
- 2 oz. soft goat cheese
- 2 Tbsp. sesame, sunflower and chia seeds, lightly toasted on a dry pan over a low heat

## Directions:

1. Preheat your oven to 375 degrees Fahrenheit and line a baking tray with baking paper.
2. Place the bell pepper, zucchini, mushrooms, pumpkin and broccoli onto the tray and drizzle with olive oil, add a pinch of salt and pepper, give the veggies a massage with your hands to ensure they're coated in oil and seasoning.

3. Place them into the oven for about 25 minutes or until roasted, soft and golden.
4. While the veggies are roasting, make the cheese balls: place the cream cheese and goat cheese into a bowl, stir vigorously until smooth and combined.
5. Lay the toasted seeds onto a plate.
6. Roll the cheese mixture into balls and roll them in the seeds until coated.
7. Serve the roasted veggies with the cheese balls over the top, and an extra drizzle of olive oil.
8. Strange... but delicious!

# Dinner

## *Caprese Salad*

*One of the world's yummiest salads, the Caprese salad combines the sweetness of tomatoes, the fragrance of fresh basil, and the creamy, heavenly tastiness of fresh mozzarella cheese. All topped with a pinch of sea salt and a drizzle of olive oil.*

Serving: 2

Time: approximately 10 minutes

**Nutritional info:**

- Calories: 250
- Fat: 21 grams
- Carbs: 7 grams
- Protein: 8.6 grams

**Ingredients:**

- 2 tomatoes, sliced
- 10 fresh basil leaves
- 1 large ball of fresh mozzarella (the yummy stuff floating in liquid!), sliced or torn
- 2 Tbsp. olive oil
- 1 tsp. sea salt

**Directions:**

1. Layer the tomatoes, basil and mozzarella onto a serving plate
2. Drizzle with olive oil and sprinkle with sea salt
3. Enjoy!

**NOTE:** yes, this is a very light dinner indeed, so make sure you keep snacking throughout the day if you are exercising or engaging in lots of busy activity.

# Day 10

## Breakfast

### *Mushroom Muffins*

*These are muffins...but without the flour. In fact, they're more like little quiches, but they're made in muffin pans and baked...so muffins they are!*

*Mushrooms, spinach and zucchini give you your veggie hit, while egg and cream cheese provide creaminess and protein.*

Servings: makes 12 muffins (1 muffin per serving)

Time: approximately 20 minutes

**Nutritional info:**

- Calories: 75
- Fat: 5.8 grams
- Carbs: 2 grams
- Protein: 4 grams

**Ingredients:**

- 3 cups mixed mushrooms, sliced
- 1 medium-large zucchini, sliced
- 1 cup baby spinach leaves
- 5 eggs, lightly beaten
- Salt and pepper
- 5 oz. cream cheese, broken or cut into little pieces or chunks

**Directions:**

1. Preheat your oven to 375 degrees Fahrenheit and crease a 12-hole muffin pan.
2. Place the mushrooms, zucchini, spinach, eggs, salt and pepper into a bowl and stir to combine.
3. Pour the mixture into the muffin pan and place into the oven.

4. Bake for about 12-15 minutes or until just set.
5. Make the cream cheese frosting by simply stirring the cream cheese to loosen it and bring it to a spreadable consistency.
6. Allow the cooked muffins to cool before frosting with cream cheese!

# Lunch

## *Keto Pizza*

*Pizza! Well, keto pizza. The base is made from cauliflower, almond meal and egg, and topped with cheese, tomato and basil. Classic. Delicious.*

Servings: makes 1 medium-sized pizza (2 servings per pizza)

Time: approximately 30 minutes

### Nutritional info:

- Calories: 500
- Fat: 35.5 grams
- Carbs: 17.5 grams
- Protein: 31 grams

### Ingredients:

- 1 cauliflower head, blitzed in a food processor until it resembles fine grains
- ½ cup ground almonds (almond flour)
- 2 eggs, lightly beaten
- Salt and pepper
- 1 cup tomato puree (passata, or canned tomatoes, no sugar or flavors added)
- 1 cup grated cheddar
- 2 oz. mozzarella cheese
- 10 fresh basil leaves

### Directions:

1. Preheat the oven to 375 degrees Fahrenheit and line a baking tray or pizza stone with baking paper.
2. In a large bowl, mix together the blitzed cauliflower, ground almonds, eggs, salt and pepper until it forms a thick dough, if it's too dry, add a drop or two of water to bring it together.
3. Press the pizza "dough" out onto your lined baking tray and shape into a rough circle.

63

4.  Place the tray into the oven and bake for about 5 minutes, just to give the dough a chance to cook before the toppings go on.
5.  Take the tray out of the oven and spread the tomato puree over the base.
6.  Sprinkle cheddar over the tomato, lay the basil leaves over the cheddar, then finish with the mozzarella.
7.  Bake the pizza in the oven for about 12 minutes or until the cheese is bubbly and the crust is golden.

# Dinner

## *Stuffed Zucchinis*

*Zucchinis are a great vessel for tasty ingredients. Once you scoop the seeds out, you fill the "shells" with veggies, cheese and nuts, then throw them in the oven to bake!*

Serving: 2

Time: approximately 30 minutes

### Nutritional info:

- Calories: 420
- Fat: 25.8 grams
- Carbs: 15 grams
- Protein: 10 grams

### Ingredients:

- 2 large zucchinis, cut in half, lengthways, seeds scooped out with a spoon
- 1 cup canned tomatoes (the chopped ones!)
- ¾ cup grated cheese (use what you've got, I usually use cheddar)
- ¼ cup walnuts
- 2 large Portobello mushrooms, finely chopped
- 1 garlic clove, minced or finely chopped
- 2 Tbsp. olive oil
- Salt and pepper

### Directions:

1. Preheat your oven to 400 degrees Fahrenheit and line a baking tray with baking paper, lay the halved zucchinis onto the tray.
2. In a medium-sized bowl, mix together the tomatoes, cheese, walnuts, chopped mushrooms and garlic until combined.
3. Spoon the mixture into the halved zucchinis and drizzle over the olive oil.
4. Sprinkle with salt and pepper.
5. Place the tray into the oven and bake for about 25 minutes or until bubbling and golden.
6. Enjoy

# Day 11

## Breakfast

### *Overnight Oats with Chia and Almond Essence*

*Don't worry, there's only a very tiny amount of oats in this recipe. The rest is made from chia seeds which provide amazing fiber to keep you full. If you don't have almond essence, simply leave it out, it will still taste amazing.*

Servings: 1

Time: 5 minutes to prep, plus leaving overnight

## Nutritional info:

- Calories: 240
- Fat: 15.2 grams
- Carbs:  18 grams
- Protein: 8 grams

## Ingredients:

- 1 Tbsp. whole oats
- 2 Tbsp. chia seeds
- 1 cup coconut milk (or your favorite non-dairy milk)
- 1 tsp. vanilla extract
- ¼ tsp. almond extract
- 1 Tbsp. slivered almonds

## Directions:

1. Combine all ingredients in a small bowl.
2. Cover and place into the fridge until the next morning.
3. In the morning, you might want to add a dash or two of your favorite milk to loosen the consistency as it can tend to become quite stiff overnight, it's up to you!
4. Enjoy with a hot cup of coffee.

# Lunch

## *Stuffed Peppers with Mushroom, Goat Cheese and Paprika Filling*

*Yup, another "stuffed" recipe! I find stuffed veggies to be easy, fun and a little bit fancy. These peppers are stuffed with mushrooms, goat cheese and a pinch of paprika for smokiness.*

Servings: 4

Time: approximately 30 minutes

### Nutritional info:

- Calories: 130
- Fat: 8.2 grams
- Carbs: 8 grams
- Protein: 6 grams

### Ingredients:

- 2 large red bell peppers, sliced in half, seeds removed
- 2 large Portobello mushrooms, finely chopped
- 3 oz. goat cheese (or feta), crumbled
- ½ red onion, finely chopped
- 1 garlic clove, finely chopped
- 1 cup baby spinach, roughly chopped
- 1 tsp. paprika
- 1 Tbsp. olive oil
- Salt and pepper

### Directions:

1. Preheat the oven to 375 degrees Fahrenheit and line a baking tray with baking paper.
2. Place the bell pepper halves onto the tray.
3. In a small bowl, combine the mushrooms, cheese, onion, garlic, spinach, paprika, olive oil, salt and pepper.

4. Spoon the filling into the peppers and drizzle over some extra olive oil and sprinkle over a pinch more salt and pepper.
5. Bake in the preheated oven for approximately 25 minutes or until golden, soft and bubbling.
6. Enjoy!

**NOTE:** sometimes I add a little dollop of plain Greek yogurt on top for extra creaminess and a cooling contrast to the hot filling.

# Dinner

## *Eggplant burgers*

*These burgers feature eggplant buns and keto/veggie-friendly patties made from veggies, egg and almond flour. Dress with mayo, cheese and salad. Amazing.*

Serving: 2

Time:  approximately 40 minutes

## Nutritional info:

- Calories: 560
- Fat: 52 grams
- Carbs: 15 grams
- Protein: 21 grams

## Ingredients:

- 1 large eggplant, sliced along the width (so you get circular disks) into 8 slices
- 2 Tbsp. olive oil (to brush onto the eggplant)
- 2 eggs
- ½ cup almond flour
- 2 large Portobello mushrooms, finely chopped
- 1 cup pumpkin, cubed and cooked in the microwave until soft (remove the skins first)
- 1 tsp. chili powder
- ½ tsp. ground cumin
- ½ tsp. paprika
- Salt and pepper
- Olive oil
- 2 Tbsp. mayonnaise
- 2 slices cheddar cheese
- 1 tomato, sliced
- 2 iceberg lettuce leaves

## Directions:

1. Brush the eggplant slices with olive oil and leave aside as you prepare the patties.
2. In a large bowl, combine the eggs, almond flour, mushrooms. pumpkin, chili, cumin, paprika, salt and pepper until combined and smooth.
3. Heat a frying pan over a medium-high heat and add a drizzle of olive oil.
4. Once the pan is hot, fry the eggplant slices on both sides until golden, leave aside.
5. Roll the burger mixture into patties and fry on both sides until golden.
6. Assemble your burgers with a burger patty, mayo, cheese, tomato and lettuce, sandwiched between 2 eggplant "buns"!

# Day 12

## Breakfast

### *Coconut Coffee Smoothie*

*I don't know about you, but sometimes I can't quite face a full-on breakfast. But I can always manage a smoothie...especially if it involves coffee. This smoothie is refreshing, yummy and easy to drink on-the-go if you're in a hurry.*

Servings: 1

Time: approximately 10 minutes

**Nutritional info:**

- Calories: 105
- Fat: 5 grams
- Carbs: 5 grams
- Protein: 9 grams

**Ingredients:**

- 1 cup coconut milk
- ½ cup full-fat Greek yogurt
- 1 tsp. instant coffee, dissolved in a small dash of boiling water (about 1 Tbsp)
- 1 tsp. vanilla extract
- Handful of ice
- A few drops of stevia if you prefer a sweeter smoothie

**Directions:**

Place all of the ingredients into a blender and blitz until smooth!

**NOTE:** you can add all kinds of essences and extracts to your smoothies to adjust the flavor. Peppermint essence, almond essence...as long as you only use a little dash or a few drops, it won't ruin your keto journey! Get creative.

# Lunch

## *Bok Choy Sesame Stir Fry*

*Bok choy is a low-carb vegetable which is delicious when stir-fried with sesame seeds, soy sauce and a spritz of lime.*

Servings: 2

Time: approximately 15 minutes

**Nutritional info:**

- Calories: 260
- Fat: 21 grams
- Carbs: 9.5 grams
- Protein: 10 grams

**Ingredients:**

- 2 large bunches of bok choy, core cut off and leaves rinsed
- 1 Tbsp. sesame seeds
- 1 Tbsp. sesame oil
- 1 Tbsp. olive oil
- 2 Tbsp. low-carb soy sauce
- 2 eggs

**Directions:**

1. Place a frying pan over a medium heat.
2. Once the pan is hot, add the sesame seeds and toast until golden.
3. Add the sesame oil, olive oil and soy sauce, bring to a simmer.
4. Add the bok choy and stir to coat in oil and soy sauce.
5. Keep stirring the bok choy as it cooks and wilts.
6. Once the bok choy is cooked, remove it from the pan and set aside.
7. Crack the eggs into the pan and scramble them in the remaining oil and soy sauce until just set.
8. Spoon the scrambled eggs over the bok choy before serving.

# Dinner

## *Low-Carb Veggie Curry*

*Veggie curry is creamy, spicy, nutritious and can be made with any low-carb veggies in season. This version uses bell peppers, mushrooms, broccoli and zucchini. The freezer is a great resource for dishes like this, as frozen veggies are just as good as fresh ones when you're in a pinch and can't get to the supermarket.*

Serving: 4

Time: approximately 40 minutes

### Nutritional info:

- Calories: 315
- Fat: 27 grams
- Carbs: 14 grams
- Protein: 5 grams

### Ingredients:

- 2 Tbsp. olive oil or coconut oil
- 2 Tbsp. curry paste (green, yellow or red)
- 2 bell peppers, seeds removed, sliced
- 1 cup sliced mushrooms (any variety)
- 2 cups broccoli florets
- 1 large zucchini, sliced
- 2 cups full-fat coconut cream
- 2 cups vegetable broth (stock)
- Fresh cilantro and fresh red chili to garnish

### Directions:

1. Drizzle the oil into a large frying pan and place over a medium heat.
2. Once the oil is hot, add the curry paste and stir as the paste becomes fragrant.
3. Add the bell peppers, mushrooms, broccoli and zucchini, stir to coat in curry paste.
4. Add the coconut cream and broth, stir to combine.

5. Bring to a simmer and cook until the broccoli just cooked but still crunchy.
6. Transfer to bowls and sprinkle the cilantro and red chili over the top.

**NOTE:** this is more of a thin, soupy curry than a gravy-based curry.

# Day 13

## Breakfast

### *Cottage Cheese Hotcakes with Almond Butter*

*These pancakes have cottage cheese AND ricotta cheese...double the creaminess. Almond flour and coconut flour provide body, while eggs bind it all together. A dollop of almond butter adds more good fat.*

Servings: 2

Time: approximately 25 minutes

### Nutritional info:

- Calories: 690
- Fat: 48.5 grams
- Carbs: 24.5 grams
- Protein: 40 grams

### Ingredients:

- 1 cup full-fat cottage cheese
- ½ cup full-fat ricotta cheese
- 2 eggs
- ¼ cup cream or coconut cream
- ½ cup ground almonds
- ⅓ cup coconut flour
- ½ tsp. baking powder
- 1 tsp. vanilla extract
- Butter for frying
- 2 tsp. almond butter (1 tsp. per serving)

### Directions:

1. Place the cottage cheese, ricotta cheese, eggs and cream/coconut cream into a bowl, whisk until smooth.

2. Add the ground almonds, coconut flour, baking powder and vanilla extract, whisk until smooth.
3. Place a non-stick frying pan over a medium heat and add a little knob of butter.
4. Once the butter has melted, add dollops of batter onto the hot pan.
5. Once you see bubbles appearing, flip the pancakes over.
6. Serve with your almond butter and enjoy!

# Lunch

## *Celery Boats with Nut Butter (Snack)*

*Since we had a pretty heavy breakfast and we are having a decadent dinner, lunch is really light. Celery is a great keto veggie, especially when slathered with nut butter.*

Servings: 1

Time: approximately 5 minutes

### Nutritional info:

- Calories: 120
- Fat: 9 grams
- Carbs: 5 grams
- Protein: 4 grams

### Ingredients:

- 2 long celery sticks, cut into 4 pieces each
- 1 Tbsp. nut butter, almond is best

### Directions:

Pack your celery and nut butter into separate containers and simply spread the nut butter onto the celery sticks when it's time to eat!

**Note:** I know this is BARELY even a recipe! But sometimes the best keto meals and snacks are the simplest.

# Dinner

## *Keto Veggie Lasagna*

*Lasagna time! This has lots of veggies, tomato puree and cheese. Great for a Friday or Saturday night dinner when you feel like something more comforting than the average weeknight meal.*

Serving: about 8 servings

Time: approximately 45 minutes

**Nutritional info:**

- Calories: 270
- Fat: 17 grams
- Carbs: 10 grams
- Protein: 4 grams

**Ingredients:**

- 2 eggplants, sliced along the width
- 2 Tbsp. olive oil (to coat the eggplant)
- 2 zucchinis, sliced lengthways
- 2 cups pumpkin, cubed, cooked in the microwave until just soft
- ½ onion
- 2 Tbsp. olive oil
- 2 cups canned chopped tomatoes
- 1 tsp. dried mixed herbs
- Salt and pepper
- 2 cups grated cheese (use any kind of cheese)
- ¾ cup full-fat cream
- Fresh basil

**Directions:**

1. Preheat the oven to 400 degrees Fahrenheit and grease a lasagna dish with olive oil.

2. Brush the eggplant slices with olive oil and place into a frying pan over a medium heat, fry on both sides until just golden.
3. Remove the eggplant from the pan and set aside.
4. Keep the pan over the heat, add the onion, olive oil, tomatoes, mixed herbs, salt and pepper, bring to a simmer and allow to bubble away for about 10 minutes.
5. As the tomato sauce is bubbling, place the grated cheese and cream into a small pot over a low heat and stir as it gently melts together.
6. Layer the eggplant, zucchini, pumpkin and tomato sauce (about 2 sets of layers in this order), then pour the cheese/cream mixture over the top.
7. Place into the oven and back for approximately 30 minutes until bubbling and golden.

# Day 14

## Breakfast

### *Cauliflower Toast with Avocado*

*Thank god for the cauliflower. It can be made into rice AND toast! Bound together with egg and flavored with cheese, it really is tasty. Top it off with creamy avocado and a drizzle of olive oil.*

Servings: 4

Time: approximately 30 minutes

**Nutritional info:**

- Calories: 220
- Fat: 10.5 grams
- Carbs: 9 grams
- Protein: 8 grams

**Ingredients:**

- 1 small-medium cauliflower, blitzed in a food processor until very fine
- 2 eggs
- 1 cup grated cheese
- Salt and pepper
- 1 avocado
- 2 tsp. olive oil

**Directions:**

1. Preheat the oven to 400 degrees Fahrenheit and line a baking tray with baking paper.
2. Place the blitzed cauliflower into a microwave-safe bowl with a dash of water and cook in the microwave for about 7 minutes.

3. Let the cauliflower cool down slightly before tipping out into a muslin cloth or tea towel, squeeze it over the sink until all of the moisture has been drained off, place the cauliflower back into the bowl.
4. Add the eggs, cheese, salt and pepper, stir to thoroughly combine.
5. Press the mixture into squares onto your lined baking tray, make sure you press them tight.
6. Place the tray into the oven and bake for about 20 minutes or until golden brown.
7. Top with avocado, olive oil and a pinch of salt and pepper!

# Lunch

## *Fat-bomb Smoothie*

*This smoothie feels kind of like dessert...which totally works for me! When you are having major chocolate cravings, this is the perfect lunch to get your fix. Good fats, (and some more decadent fats), chocolate and a hint of cinnamon.*

Servings: 2

Time: approximately 10 minutes

## Nutritional info:

- Calories: 610
- Fat: 40 grams
- Carbs: 6.5 grams
- Protein: 2 grams

## Ingredients:

- ½ cup full fat cream
- 1 cup full fat coconut milk
- 1 cup almond milk
- 2 Tbsp. flaxseed oil
- 3 oz. dark chocolate (melted)
- 1 tsp. cinnamon
- 1 cup ice

## Directions:

1. Place all ingredients into a blender and blitz until smooth!
2. Enjoy!

# Dinner

## *Grilled Cheese Sandwiches (with Zucchini Bread)*

*Grilled cheese sandwiches are, in my opinion, just as yummy when made with zucchini bread. It's kind of like a sandwich made with zucchini omelets, with hot melted cheese oozing out... incredible.*

Servings: 3

Time: approximately 25 minutes

### Nutritional info:

- Calories: 330
- Fat: 27 grams
- Carbs: 8 grams
- Protein: 15 grams

### Ingredients:

- 2 zucchinis, grated, then squeezed over the sink to remove all of the moisture
- 1 egg
- 1 garlic clove, minced or finely chopped
- ½ cup ground almonds
- Salt and pepper
- Olive oil for frying
- 3 thick slices of cheese (mozzarella or cheddar)

### Directions:

1. Place the grated, squeezed zucchini into a bowl and add the egg, garlic, almonds, salt and pepper, stir to thoroughly combine.
2. Place a non-stick frying pan over a medium heat and drizzle with olive oil.
3. Once the pan is hot, spread a dollop of mixture onto the pan and leave to cook slightly before laying a layer of cheese on top.
4. Once the cheese has melted slightly, cover it with another layer of zucchini mixture and continue to cook.
5. Once you feel that the bottom layer is cooked, carefully flip the sandwich over and cook until both sides are golden and the cheese has melted.
6. Eat while hot or warm!

# Day 15

## Breakfast

### *Keto-Friendly Porridge*

*I haven't called this "oatmeal" because it doesn't have any oats. Instead, it has seeds cooked in butter and coconut cream.*

Servings: 1

Time: approximately 20 minutes

**Nutritional info:**

- Calories: 410
- Fat: 38 grams
- Carbs: 10 grams
- Protein: 6.6 grams

**Ingredients:**

- 1 Tbsp. chia seeds
- 1 Tbsp. ground flaxseed
- 1/3 cup coconut cream
- ½ cup water
- 1 tsp. vanilla extract
- 1 Tbsp. butter

**Directions:**

1. Place the chia seeds, flaxseed, coconut cream, water and vanilla into a small pot, stir, and leave for about 5 minutes to allow the chia seeds to hydrate.
2. Add the butter and place the pot over a low heat, stirring as the butter melts and the mixture thickens.
3. Once the porridge is hot but not boiling, pour into a bowl and enjoy!
4. You can add a few berries and a dash of cream for an extra-decadent breakfast.

# Lunch

## *Fried Tempeh Salad*

*Tempeh is like tofu but firmer and becomes almost like fries when cooked in olive oil in a hot pan. A fresh salad accented with crispy, fried morsels!*

Servings: 4

Time: approximately 25 minutes

### Nutritional info:

- Calories: 300
- Fat: 23.5 grams
- Carbs: 12 grams
- Protein: 13 grams

### Ingredients:

- 3 Tbsp. olive oil
- 8 oz. tempeh, cut into slices
- 4 cups lettuce, shredded
- 1 tomato, cut into wedges
- ½ cucumber, cut into small chunks
- 1 avocado, cut into chunks
- 3 oz. feta cheese, cut into small pieces
- 1 Tbsp. pumpkin seeds
- 1 Tbsp. olive oil
- 1 Tbsp. apple cider vinegar

### Directions:

1. Pour the olive oil into a frying pan and place over a medium-high heat.
2. Once the oil is hot, very carefully place the tempeh into the oil and turn a few times as it fries, until the pieces are golden on all sides.
3. In a large bowl, place the lettuce, tomato, cucumber, avocado, feta and pumpkin seeds, toss to combine.
4. Combine the olive oil and apple cider vinegar and drizzle it over the salad, toss to combine.
5. Scatter the fried tempeh over the salad before serving!

# Dinner

## *Keto Nachos*

*Look, there's no way that we can have proper tortilla chips, but we can have bell peppers. Shards of bell pepper are a great vessel for cheese, tomato, spices and jalapenos.*

Servings: 4

Time: approximately 30 minutes

## Nutritional info:

- Calories: 190
- Fat: 8.5 grams
- Carbs: 9 grams
- Protein: 3.8 grams

## Ingredients:

- 4 bell peppers (red ones are best), seeds removed, cut into about 8 wedges each
- 2 Tbsp. olive oil
- 1 tsp. ground cumin
- 1 tsp. paprika
- 1 tsp. ground chili
- 1 tsp. garlic powder
- Salt and pepper
- ½ onion, finely chopped
- 1 tomato, finely chopped (you can drain some of the liquid away so it doesn't become soggy)
- 2 Tbsp. chopped jalapenos
- 1 cup grated cheddar cheese

## Directions:

1. Preheat the oven to 400 degrees Fahrenheit and line a baking tray with baking paper.

2. Lay the bell pepper wedges onto the lined tray and drizzle with olive oil.
3. Combine the cumin, paprika, chili, garlic powder, salt and pepper in a cup and sprinkle the mixture over the bell pepper wedges.
4. Combine the onion, tomato and jalapenos in a small bowl and spoon the mixture over the bell pepper wedges.
5. Sprinkle the cheese over the top of the wedges and place the tray into the oven.
6. Bake for 10 - 12 minutes or until the cheese is golden and bubbling!.

# Day 16

## Breakfast

### *Chocolate Bombs*

*This is another "on the go" breakfast for when you feel like a nibble rather than a meal. Cocoa, almond butter and coconut oil provide the "chocolatey", fatty goodness!*

Servings: makes 12 balls, 2 balls per serving

Time: approximately 10 minutes to prepare, then about an hour to refrigerate until ready to eat

**Nutritional info:**

- Calories: 555
- Fat: 55 grams
- Carbs: 11.5 grams
- Protein: 11 grams

**Ingredients:**

- ¾ cup coconut oil
- 1 cup almond butter
- 1/3 cup cocoa powder (unsweetened)
- ¼ cup ground almonds
- ½ tsp. sea salt
- Stevia if you want a sweeter treat

**Directions:**

1. Place all ingredients into a pot and place over a low heat, stir as the mixture melts together.
2. Once the mixture has combined to form a thick batter, take the pot off the heat and leave to cool.
3. Roll the mixture into balls and place on a paper-lined baking tray.
4. Place the tray into the fridge and allow the balls to cool and set for about an hour before eating or transferring to an airtight container.

# Lunch

## *Creamy Pesto Pasta (Zoodles)*

*Ah, the everlasting trend that is the "zoodle". Zucchinis shredded into noodle-like strips, coated in creamy, tasty sauces... just like pasta but without the carbs and the ketosis-busting consequences.*

Servings: 2

Time: approximately 30 minutes

## Nutritional info:

- Calories: 420
- Fat: 35.5 grams
- Carbs: 16 grams
- Protein: 12 grams

## Ingredients:

- 1 Tbsp. olive oil
- 4 large zucchinis, turned into zoodles either with a spiralizer or a sharp knife and lots of patience!
- 3 Tbsp. basil pesto (store-bought is fine, just make sure it only contains basil, Parmesan and pine nuts)
- 4 Tbsp. heavy cream
- 2 oz. Parmesan cheese (I don't weigh it, I just grate it over the pasta, it's probably far less than an ounce per serving but I've accounted for an ounce just to be safe with macros)

## Directions:

1. Drizzle the olive oil into a frying pan and place over a medium heat.
2. Once the oil is hot, add the zoodles and stir gently as they cook, about 3 minutes.
3. Add the pesto and stir to coat the zoodles.
4. Turn the heat off, add the cream and stir to combine until the zoodles are all coated in pesto and cream.
5. Grate the Parmesan cheese over the hot zoodles right before serving!

# Dinner

## *Roasted Cauliflower Salad*

*Cauliflower, as you can tell by now, is a ketogenic staple. When it is roasted, it takes on an almost nutty, baked flavor which I adore. This salad is doused in olive oil, lemon juice, and scattered with scallions, walnuts and feta cheese.*

Servings: 4

Time: approximately 40 minutes

**Nutritional info:**

- Calories: 270
- Fat: 22.6 grams
- Carbs: 9 grams
- Protein: 9.3 grams

**Ingredients:**

- 1 large cauliflower head, cut into florets
- 2 Tbsp. olive oil
- Salt and pepper
- 1 tsp. chili powder
- 3 Tbsp. finely chopped scallions
- 3 Tbsp. roughly chopped walnuts
- 4 oz. feta cheese, chopped into small chunks
- 2 Tbsp. olive oil
- Juice of one lemon

**Directions:**

1. Preheat the oven to 400 degrees Fahrenheit and line a baking tray with baking paper.
2. Lay the cauliflower florets onto the tray and drizzle with olive oil, salt, pepper and chili powder.
3. Roast in the oven for approximately 30 minutes or until golden.
4. Transfer the roasted cauliflower into bowl and add the scallions, walnuts, feta, olive oil and lemon juice, toss to combine.
5. Serve and eat!

# Day 17

## Breakfast

### *Avocado Berry Smoothie*

*Another smoothie! This smoothie is creamy, thick and full of nutrients. The cream seems indulgent, but on keto... cream is a completely valid ingredient for any meal.*

Servings: 4

Time: approximately 10 minutes

## Nutritional info:

- Calories: 270
- Fat: 23.5 grams
- Carbs: 10 grams
- Protein: 6 grams

## Ingredients:

- 1 avocado, flesh scooped out
- 2 Tbsp. flaxseed oil
- 1 cup mixed frozen berries (raspberries, strawberries and blueberries are great)
- 1 cup full-fat Greek yoghurt
- ½ cup full-fat cream
- ½ Tbsp. cocoa powder (optional, but I just love the combo of berries and cocoa)
- 1 cup ice

## Directions:

1. Place all ingredients into a blender and blend until smooth
2. Pour into a tall glass or bottle and sip away!

# Lunch

## *Mac and Cheese (Veggie-Keto Style)*

*It's true, there is technically no "mac" in this mac and cheese, but the mac is replaced by broccoli and cauliflower (if you just can't bear another cauliflower, feel free to use broccoli for the whole recipe!).*

Servings: 4

Time: approximately 40 minutes

### Nutritional info:

- Calories: 380
- Fat: 26 grams
- Carbs: 10 grams
- Protein: 10 grams

### Ingredients:

- ½ cauliflower, cut into florets
- 1 small-medium broccoli, cut into florets
- 1 garlic clove, minced or finely chopped
- ½ cup creme fraiche
- ½ cup cottage cheese
- ½ cup heavy cream
- 1 cup grated cheddar
- Salt and pepper

### Directions:

1. Preheat the oven to 400 degrees Fahrenheit and grease a medium-sized baking dish with olive oil.
2. Place the cauliflower and broccoli into a microwave-safe bowl with a dash of water, microwave for 1-minute increments until the veggies are JUST cooked but still crunchy, do not overcook.

3. Place the garlic, creme fraiche, cottage cheese, cream, cheddar, salt and pepper into a pot and place over a low-medium heat, stir as the mixture melts together and becomes smooth.
4. Tip the cauliflower and broccoli into the pot of creamy sauce and stir to combine.
5. Pour the mixture into your prepared dish and place into the preheated oven.
6. Bake for about 30 minutes or until golden and bubbling.
7. Eat while hot!

# Dinner

## *Quesadillas*

*Mexican-inspired dinner! These quesadillas are made from an omelet-style wrap, with creme fraiche and avocado.*

Servings: 4

Time: approximately

### Nutritional info:

- Calories: 380
- Fat: 26 grams
- Carbs: 7.5 grams
- Protein: 11 grams

### Ingredients:

- 4 eggs
- ½ cup cream cheese
- 2 Tbsp. ground almonds
- ½ tsp. ground cumin
- Salt and pepper
- Drizzle of olive oil for frying
- 1 cup grated cheddar cheese
- 1 avocado, flesh removed
- 1 large tomato, cut into small cubes
- 2 Tbsp. scallions
- 1 tsp. ground chili
- 4 Tbsp. creme fraiche

### Directions:

1. Place the eggs, cream cheese, ground almonds, cumin, salt and pepper into a bowl and whisk until smooth.

2. Heat a non-stick frying pan over a medium heat and drizzle some olive oil into the pan.
3. Pour the egg batter into the hot pan so it forms a thin pancake.
4. Once you see bubbles appearing, carefully flip the pancake over until both sides are golden.
5. Continue until all of the batter has been cooked.
6. Place one cooked pancake back onto the hot pan and sprinkle some grated cheese over the top, place another pancake on top and cook until the cheese has melted.
7. Place the quesadilla onto a board and slice into wedges.
8. Serve with tomatoes, avocado, scallions, creme fraiche and a pinch of ground chili over the top.

# Day 18

## Breakfast

### *Smoothie Bowl*

*This is a beautiful breakfast...literally, the colors are glorious. Filled with fiber, greens and good fats. Jump on the smoothie-bowl bandwagon and enjoy!*

Servings: 2

Time: approximately 10 minutes

**Nutritional info:**

- Calories: 380
- Fat: 36 grams
- Carbs: 12 grams
- Protein: 5 grams

**Ingredients:**

- 2 cups baby spinach leaves
- 1 cup coconut milk (or almond milk)
- ¼ cup heavy cream
- 2 Tbsp. flaxseed oil
- 2 Tbsp. chia seeds
- 2 Tbsp. roughly chopped walnuts
- A handful of fresh berries (any, but I always go for raspberries)

**Directions:**

1. Place the spinach leaves, coconut milk, cream and flaxseed oil into a blender and blitz until smooth.
2. Pour the smoothie into two bowls.
3. Sprinkle the chia seeds, walnuts and berries over the top before serving.
4. Eat!

# Lunch

## *Tomato and Bell Pepper Soup*

*Some people consider nightshades (pepper and tomatoes included) to be veggies which must be eaten in small amounts. However, I think that since we are on such a restricted diet, we should take a few liberties and eat as many low-carb veggies as we want, as long as they are in our macro guidelines. This is a tasty, tangy, silky soup.*

Servings: 4

Time: approximately 35 minutes

### Nutritional info:

- Calories: 270
- Fat: 22 grams
- Carbs: 16 grams
- Protein: 3.5 grams

### Ingredients:

- 4 bell peppers, red, orange or yellow, seeds removed, roughly chopped
- 3 large tomatoes, cut into chunks
- 1 cup pumpkin, cubed, (this helps to thicken the soup and create a creamy texture)
- 2 garlic cloves, roughly chopped
- 3 cups veggie broth (stock)
- Salt and pepper
- 1 cup heavy cream

### Directions:

1. Place the peppers, tomatoes, pumpkin, garlic, broth, salt and pepper into a large pot over a medium-high heat.
2. Bring to the boil and leave covered to boil for approximately 25 minutes or until the veggies are very soft.
3. With a handheld stick blender, blitz the soup until smooth.
4. Add the cream and stir to combine before serving.

# Dinner

## *Fresh, Tangy Slaw*

*This is a fresh slaw with a hit of saltiness and a creamy, yogurt-based dressing. A tiny addition of apple adds sweetness and extra crunch.*

Servings: 4

Time: approximately 15 minutes

## Nutritional info:

- Calories: 130
- Fat: 9 grams
- Carbs: 9.5 grams
- Protein: 4 grams

## Ingredients:

- ½ red cabbage, shredded
- ½ green cabbage, shredded
- ½ apple, grated
- 3 Tbsp. finely chopped scallions
- 2 Tbsp. pumpkin seeds
- 1/3 cup full-fat Greek yoghurt
- 2 Tbsp. apple cider vinegar
- 2 Tbsp. olive oil
- Salt and pepper

## Directions:

1. Place the red cabbage, green cabbage, apple, scallions, pumpkin seeds, yogurt, apple cider vinegar, salt and pepper into a bowl, toss to thoroughly combine, make sure everything is evenly coated in yoghurt, vinegar and oil.
2. Serve.
3. Yes, it's that simple!

# I

## B

### *Keto*

*This is a recipe for people who really h*
*not often one of these people. I usually*
*plenty of people who aren't ready to eat u*
*is hit with butter, cinnamon an*

*Roasted*

*Green beans are amazing*

Servings: 2

Time: approx

Nut

Servings: 2

Time: approximately 10 minutes

## Nutritional info:

- Calories: 160
- Fat: 17.5 grams
- Carbs: 1 gram
- Protein: .5 gram

## Ingredients:

- 2 cups hot coffee, however you like to make it, I use plunger coffee
- 2 Tbsp. butter
- ½ tsp. cinnamon
- 1 tsp. cocoa powder
- 2 Tbsp. cream
- A few drops of stevia if you prefer a sweeter coffee

## Directions:

1. Pour the coffee into a pot and add the butter, cinnamon, cocoa, cream and stevia, place the pot over a low-medium heat.
2. Bring to a gentle simmer until the butter has melted.
3. Pour into two coffee cups and enjoy!

# Lunch

## *reen Bean and Arugula Salad*

*when roasted, and even better when tossed into a peppery, citrusy arugula salad.*

mately 30 minutes

**tional info:**

- Calories: 520
- Fat: 45 grams
- Carbs: 11.8 grams
- Protein: 27 grams

## Ingredients:

- 4 oz. fresh green beans
- 2 Tbsp. olive oil
- 2 oz. Parmesan cheese, finely grated
- 1 garlic clove, minced or finely chopped
- Salt and pepper
- 4 cups arugula
- ½ cucumber, chopped into chunks
- 2 Tbsp. sunflower seeds, dry toasted in a hot pan until golden
- 3 oz. goat cheese, cut into small chunks
- 1 Tbsp. olive oil
- Juice of 1 lemon

## Directions:

1. Preheat the 375 degrees Fahrenheit and line a baking tray with baking paper
2. Spread the beans onto the lined baking tray and drizzle over the olive oil, sprinkle over the Parmesan cheese, garlic, salt and pepper, stir until the beans are evenly coated

3. Place the tray into the oven and cook for about 20 minutes or until the beans are golden
4. Place the arugula, cucumber, sunflower seeds, goat cheese and roasted beans into a bowl, drizzle over the olive oil and lemon juice, toss to combine
5. Serve and eat!

# Dinner

## *Spicy Fried Halloumi with Cabbage and Fresh Chili*

*This is a really interesting mixture of ingredients, but it's surprisingly delicious. Halloumi is salty and creamy, the cabbage is crunchy, and the chili is gloriously hot.*

Servings: 4

Time: approximately 20 minutes

### Nutritional info:

- Calories: 280
- Fat: 23.5 grams
- Carbs: 3.5 grams
- Protein: 14 grams

### Ingredients:

- 8 oz. halloumi cheese, sliced
- ½ green cabbage, shredded
- 2 Tbsp. scallions
- 2 Tbsp. olive oil
- 1 Tbsp. soy sauce
- ½ tsp. sesame oil
- ½ fresh red chili, finely chopped
- Salt and pepper

### Directions:

1. Heat a non-stick pan over a medium heat.
2. Once the pan is hot, place the halloumi slices onto the hot surface and fry on both sides until golden.
3. Place the cabbage, scallions, olive oil, soy sauce, sesame oil, chili, salt and pepper, toss to combine.
4. Place the cooked halloumi over the salad before serving.

# Day 20

## Breakfast

### *Refreshing Mint, Turmeric and Citrus Smoothie*

*This smoothie is golden, minty, fruity and delicious. The Greek yogurt adds protein, creaminess and thickness.*

Servings: 2

Time: approximately 10 minutes

## Nutritional info:

- Calories: 420
- Fat: 35.5 grams
- Carbs: 20 grams
- Protein: 12 grams

## Ingredients:

- Small handful of fresh mint leaves, woody stems removed
- 1 tsp. ground turmeric
- 1 orange
- 1 lemon
- 1 cup full-fat Greek yoghurt
- ½ cup heavy cream
- 1 Tbsp. flaxseed oil
- 1 cup ice

## Directions:

1. Place all ingredients into a blender and blitz until smooth
2. Pour into tall glasses and sip!

# Lunch

## *Buddha Bowl with Tofu*

*I'm trying to be trendy by calling this a "Buddha bowl", but in fact, it's just a bowl of amazing, fresh veggies, sesame seeds, and sticky tofu. Call it what you like!*

Servings: 2

Time: approximately 25 minutes

## Nutritional info:

- Calories: 180
- Fat: 13.5 grams
- Carbs: 10 grams
- Protein: 7 grams

## Ingredients:

- 8 oz. firm tofu, cut into slices
- 2 Tbsp. soy sauce
- 1 Tbsp. sesame oil
- 2 Tbsp. sesame seeds, toasted on a dry, hot pan until golden
- 1 carrot, peeled and cut into thin strips
- 1 red bell pepper, seeds removed, sliced
- 2 cups lettuce, shredded
- 1 avocado, flesh cut into chunks
- Juice of 1 lime

## Directions:

1. Place a frying pan over a medium-high heat.
2. Place the tofu, soy sauce, sesame oil and sesame seeds onto the hot surface, stir to coat the tofu in sauce and oil.
3. Fry the tofu until golden on both sides, about 5 minutes.
4. Arrange your bowls with carrot, bell pepper, lettuce and avocado.
5. Place the hot, cooked tofu into the bowls.
6. Squeeze the lime juice over the bowls before serving.
7. Enjoy!

# Dinner

## *Fresh Salad with Walnut/Avocado Dressing*

*The star of this salad is the creamy dressing made from avocado, walnuts and yogurt. Fresh salad veggies, boiled eggs and a hit of chili make for a light and satisfying dinner.*

Servings: 4

Time: approximately 20 minutes

## Nutritional info:

- Calories: 270
- Fat: 20.5 grams
- Carbs: 12.5 grams
- Protein: 10 grams

## Ingredients:

- 3 eggs, hard boiled, peeled and quartered
- 1 avocado, flesh removed
- ¼ cup walnuts
- ½ cup full-fat Greek yogurt
- 2 Tbsp. olive oil
- Juice of 1 lemon
- Salt and pepper
- 6 cups shredded lettuce
- 2 tomatoes, cut into wedges
- ½ cucumber, cut into chunks
- ½ red onion, finely chopped
- ½ fresh red chili, finely chopped

## Directions:

1. Prepare your eggs by hard boiling them whichever way you prefer (I boil mine in a rolling boil for 8 minutes then dunk them in cold water before peeling).

2. Place the avocado, walnuts, yogurt, olive oil, juice of one lemon, salt and pepper into a food processor or blender and blitz until smooth.
3. Place the lettuce, tomatoes, cucumber, red onion and chili into a bowl, toss to combine.
4. Pour the dressing over the salad and very gently toss to coat the veggies.
5. Add the boiled egg quarters at the end so they don't get ruined when you toss the salad.
6. Enjoy!

# Day 21

## Breakfast

### *Lemon Cheesecake*

*We are being rebellious today and having cheesecake for breakfast! But because it is keto-friendly, it can totally pass as breakfast.*

*Creamy, tangy and a little bit crunchy.*

Servings: 4

Time: approximately 20 minutes

**Nutritional info:**

- Calories: 360
- Fat: 33.5 grams
- Carbs: 7 grams
- Protein: 5.5 grams

**Ingredients:**

- 1/3 cup desiccated coconut
- ½ cup ground almonds
- 1 tsp. cinnamon
- 2 Tbsp. butter, melted
- 4 oz. cream cheese
- 4 Tbsp. heavy cream
- Few drops of stevia to taste
- Grated zest and juice of 1 lemon

**Directions:**

1. Combine the coconut, ground almonds, cinnamon and melted butter in a small bowl, press the mixture into the bottom of two serving glasses.

2. Combine the cream cheese, cream, stevia, lemon zest and lemon juice in a small bowl and spoon the mixture over the coconut base in each serving dish.
3. Garnish with a little bit of lemon zest.
4. Enjoy!

# Lunch

## *Zucchini Cream Cheese Soup*

*It's green, it's smooth, it's creamy and it's a fantastic keto-friendly lunch.*

Servings: 4

Time: approximately 30 minutes

### Nutritional info:

- Calories: 250
- Fat: 18 grams
- Carbs: 17 grams
- Protein: 4 grams

### Ingredients:

- 5 large zucchinis, roughly chopped
- 1 brown onion, roughly chopped
- 4 garlic cloves, roughly chopped
- 3 cups vegetable broth (stock)
- Salt and pepper
- 3 oz. cream cheese
- ½ cup heavy cream

### Directions:

1. Place the zucchini, onion, garlic, broth, salt and pepper into a pot and bring to the boil.
2. Cover and leave to simmer until the veggies are very soft.
3. With a handheld blender, blitz the soup until very smooth.
4. Add the cream cheese and cream to the hot soup and stir as they melt into the soup and become combined.
5. Serve while hot!

# Dinner

## *Cheesy Cauli-Balls with Arugula, Parmesan and Lemon Dressing*

*We are disguising our cauliflower as cheese balls this time. They sit on a bed of fresh, leafy arugula with a grating of parmesan and a drizzle of lemon dressing.*

Servings: 2

Time: approximately 25

### Nutritional info:

- Calories: 490
- Fat: 29 grams
- Carbs: 7.5 grams
- Protein: 18.8 grams

### Ingredients:

- ½ head of cauliflower, blitzed in a food processor until the size of rice
- 1 egg
- 1 cup grated cheese
- 1 tsp. paprika
- Salt and pepper
- 1 Tbsp. olive oil
- 3 cups arugula
- 2 oz. grated Parmesan
- Juice of 1 lemon
- 1 Tbsp. flaxseed oil

### Directions:

1. Combine the cauliflower, egg, cheese, paprika, salt and pepper in a bowl until incorporated.
2. Heat a non-stick pan over a medium heat and drizzle the olive oil into the pan.
3. When the pan is hot, roll the cauliflower mixture into balls and fry them in the hot oil, turning so that all sides are golden.
4. Lay your arugula onto two serving plates and place the cauli-balls on top.
5. Grate over your Parmesan cheese, squeeze the lemon juice over, then drizzle the flaxseed oil over the top.

# Day 22

## Breakfast

### Ricotta Cheese and Berries on Keto Bagels

*These bagels are made from cream cheese, egg and almond flour.*

*Topped with ricotta cheese and fresh berries, it feels like eating cake for breakfast.*

Servings: 6 (1 bagel per serving)

Time: approximately 30 minutes

## Nutritional info:

- Calories: 260
- Fat: 20 grams
- Carbs: 7.8 grams
- Protein: 12.3 grams

## Ingredients:

- 1 cup ground almonds (almond flour)
- 1 tsp. baking powder
- 3 oz. cream cheese
- 3 eggs
- 2 tsp. vanilla extract
- 1 cup ricotta cheese
- 1 cup fresh berries

## Directions:

1. Preheat your oven to 375 degrees Fahrenheit and line a baking tray with baking paper.
2. Whisk together the almond flour, baking powder, cream cheese, eggs and vanilla extract, it might be tough at first and the almond flour might take a while to incorporate with the cream cheese, but it will eventually!

3. place mounds of batter onto your baking tray and shape into a rough bagel shape, don't worry if it's not perfect!
4. Bake for approximately 25 minutes or until golden.
5. Slice the bagels in half, spread with ricotta cheese and sprinkle with fresh berries.
6. EAT!

# Lunch

## *Spinach and Feta Tart*

*Spinach and feta sit on a "pastry" base of egg and ricotta cheese.*

*This tart can be eaten hot, warm or even cold.*

Servings: 4

Time: approximately 25 minutes

### Nutritional info:

- Calories: 375
- Fat: 27 grams
- Carbs: 10 grams
- Protein: 23.3 grams

### Ingredients:

- 4 eggs
- 1 cup full-fat ricotta cheese
- 3 Tbsp. ground almonds
- 1 tsp. baking powder
- Salt and pepper
- 2 Tbsp. olive oil
- 2 garlic cloves, finely chopped
- ½ brown onion, finely chopped
- 6 cups roughly chopped spinach
- 5 oz. feta cheese, chopped into small chunks

### Directions:

1. Preheat the oven to 375 degrees Fahrenheit and line a tart dish (or pie pan) with baking paper, or grease with butter or oil spray.
2. Combine the eggs, ricotta, ground almonds, baking powder, salt and pepper in a small bowl.

113

3. Pour the egg mixture into the lined/greased dish and place into the oven to pre-bake for about 5 minutes or until just set.
4. As the base is pre-baking, prepare the filling: drizzle the olive oil into a frying pan over a medium heat, add the garlic, onion and spinach and stir as the spinach wilts and the onions become soft and translucent.
5. Take the frying pan off the heat and stir the feta into the spinach mixture.
6. Spread the spinach mixture over the pre-baked base and place back into the oven for approximately 12 minutes or until golden and set.
7. Enjoy!

# Dinner

## *Zoodle Ramen with Butter Broth*

*It's zoodle time again! This time, the zoodles take the place of ramen.*

*The broth is tasty, salty and rich, thanks to the addition of butter.*

Servings: 4

Time: approximately 30 minutes

## Nutritional info:

- Calories: 250
- Fat: 15 grams
- Carbs: 17 grams
- Protein: 9 grams

## Ingredients:

- 6 zucchinis, use a spiralizer or a sharp knife to make zoodles
- 1 Tbsp. sesame oil
- 10 oz. firm tofu, cut into slices
- 6 cups vegetable broth (stock)
- 2 Tbsp. soy sauce
- Juice of 1 lime
- 3 Tbsp. butter
- Fresh cilantro to garnish

## Directions:

1. Prepare your zoodles whichever way you like, set aside.
2. Drizzle the sesame oil into a non-stick pan and place over a medium heat.
3. Once the oil is hot, place the tofu onto the hot surface and fry on both sides until golden.
4. Pour the vegetable broth, soy sauce, lime and butter into a large pot and bring to a simmer.

5. Add the zoodles and cook for about 5 minutes or until the zoodles are just cooked but still have a "bite" to them.
6. Divide the zoodles and broth between four bowls and place the tofu on top.
7. Sprinkle the bowls with cilantro if you wish!

# Day 23

## Breakfast

### *Sweet Potato, Egg and Spinach Hash*

*I know, sweet potato isn't the most condoned keto food, but a small amount here and there is fine!*

Servings: 2

Time: approximately 30 minutes

## Nutritional info:

- Calories: 375
- Fat: 29 grams
- Carbs: 14.5 grams
- Protein: 14 grams

## Ingredients:

- 1 cup sweet potato, cubed
- 2 Tbsp. olive oil
- 1 Tbsp. butter
- 1 cup spinach, roughly chopped
- 4 eggs, lightly beaten
- Salt and pepper

## Directions:

1. Place the sweet potato cubes into a double-boiler and steam until soft.
2. Drizzle the olive oil into a non-stick pan over medium heat.
3. Once the oil is hot, add the butter, leave to melt.
4. Add the spinach and stir to coat in butter and oil, stir as the spinach wilts.
5. Push the spinach to one side of the pan to make room for the sweet potatoes.
6. Add the sweet potatoes and mash them into the oil and butter, stir occasionally but let the sweet potatoes fry.

7. Combine the spinach and sweet potatoes together.
8. Crack the eggs into the pan and stir to scramble.
9. Sprinkle with salt and pepper.
10. When the eggs are just set, it's ready to serve!

# Lunch

## *Brussels Sprouts with Spicy Dressing and Toasted Almonds*

*These Brussels sprouts are pan-fried until slightly charred, then dressed with a tangy, spicy dressing and scattered with toasted almonds.*

Servings: 4

Time: approximately 20 minutes

## Nutritional info:

- Calories: 160
- Fat: 13.4 grams
- Carbs: 9 grams
- Protein: 3.5 grams

## Ingredients:

- 16 Brussels sprouts, cut in half
- 2 garlic cloves, finely chopped
- 3 Tbsp. olive oil
- Juice of 1 lemon
- 1 fresh red chili, finely chopped
- Handful of fresh parsley, finely chopped
- 3 Tbsp. slivered almonds, toasted in a dry pan until golden
- Salt and pepper

## Directions:

1. Drizzle the olive oil into a frying pan and place over a medium heat.
2. Add the Brussels sprouts, garlic, salt and pepper, stir to combine.
3. Stir occasionally as the Brussels sprouts fry and become crispy and slightly charred.
4. Place the fried Brussels sprouts into a bowl.
5. Add the lemon juice, chili, parsley, slivered almonds and a pinch more salt and pepper, stir to combine.
6. Serve!

# Dinner

## *Jazzed-up Carbonara (using cauliflower, mushrooms and 3 cheeses)*

*Creamy pasta is one of life's greatest culinary joys. Once again, we call on the humble cauliflower to step in for pasta. A few mushrooms and not one, not two, but three cheeses accent this lovely dish.*

Servings: 4

Time: approximately 30 minutes

### Nutritional info:

- Calories: 422
- Fat: 31 grams
- Carbs: 11 grams
- Protein: 10 grams

### Ingredients:

- 2 Tbsp. olive oil
- 6 cups cauliflower florets, cut into smaller pieces
- 1 cup sliced mushrooms
- 1 cup grated cheddar cheese
- 3 oz. cream cheese
- 1 oz. blue cheese
- ½ cup heavy cream
- Salt and pepper

### Directions:

1. Drizzle the olive oil into a frying pan over a medium heat.
2. Once the oil is hot, add the cauliflower and mushrooms, stir as they fry and become golden.
3. Add the cheddar, cream cheese, blue cheese, cream, salt and pepper.
4. Keep stirring as the cheeses melt together, add a dash more cream if the mixture is too thick for your liking.
5. Once everything has melted together, it's time to serve!

# Day 24

## Breakfast

### *Green smoothie*

*It's smoothie time again. This one is green, creamy, slightly tangy and very yummy. I always feel nourished and energized after sipping one of these beauties!*

Servings: 2

Time: approximately 10 minutes

## Nutritional info:

- Calories: 360
- Fat: 28 grams
- Carbs: 18 grams
- Protein: 13 grams

## Ingredients:

- 2 cups spinach
- 1 avocado, flesh scooped out
- 1 cup almond milk
- 2 Tbsp. coconut oil
- 1 cup Greek yogurt
- 1 Tbsp. flaxseed
- Juice of 1 lime
- Pinch of cinnamon

## Directions:

1. Place all ingredients into a blender and blitz until smooth!
2. If you find that there is not enough liquid to reach the desired consistency, simply add some water.

# Lunch

## *Keto Tabbouleh with Avocado and Yogurt*

*Tabbouleh is traditionally made with bulgur wheat, which is off-limits for us. Instead, we use a small portion of nuts which have been blitzed in a food processor. Avocado and yogurt add extra fat and energy.*

Servings: 2

Time: approximately 20 minutes

### Nutritional info:

- Calories: 215 calories
- Fat: 16.7 grams
- Carbs: 12 grams
- Protein: 6.5 grams

### Ingredients:

- ¼ cup almonds, blitzed in a food processor until they resemble couscous
- 2 cups fresh parsley, finely chopped
- 2 tomatoes, cut into small chunks
- ¼ red onion, finely chopped
- 10 fresh mint leaves, finely chopped
- 1 avocado, flesh sliced into chunks
- ½ cup Greek yogurt
- Juice of 1 lemon
- 2 Tbsp. olive oil
- Salt and pepper

### Directions:

1. Place the almonds, parsley, tomatoes, red onion, mint leaves and avocado into a bowl and gently toss to combine.
2. In a small bowl, stir together the yogurt, lemon juice, olive oil, salt and pepper until combined.

3. Pour the yogurt mixture over the tabbouleh and stir to combine.
4. Serve!

**Note:** this is also lovely as a side dish at dinner time.

# Dinner

## *Keto Chili with Sour Cream and Guacamole*

*Lots of veggies, canned tomatoes and spices are the basis for this keto-style chili. Of course, we serve it with sour cream and guacamole! If you are serving this to non-keto eaters, just throw some tortilla chips or taco wraps on their plate and they'll be smiling.*

Servings: 4

Time: approximately 30 minutes

## Nutritional info:

- Calories: 280
- Fat: 21 grams
- Carbs: 19.5 grams
- Protein: 5 grams

## Ingredients:

- 2 Tbsp. olive oil
- ½ onion, roughly chopped
- 1 tsp. paprika
- 1 tsp. ground chili
- 1 tsp. ground cumin
- 1 tsp. ground coriander (cilantro seeds)
- 2 zucchini, cut into cubes
- 3 bell peppers, (any colors), seeds removed, cut into small pieces
- 1 cup mushrooms, cut into small pieces
- 2 cups canned chopped tomatoes
- 1 avocado, mashed with salt and pepper
- ¾ cup full-fat sour cream

## Directions:

1. Drizzle the olive oil into a large frying pan or pot and place over a medium heat.

2.  When the oil is hot, add the onion, paprika, chili, cumin and ground coriander, stir as the onions cook and the spices become fragrant.
3.  Add the zucchini, bell peppers and mushrooms to the pot, stir to coat in spices, keep stirring as the veggies cook.
4.  Add the tomatoes and a good pinch of salt and pepper, stir to combine.
5.  Leave the chili to cook for about 15 minutes.
6.  Serve with guacamole and sour cream dolloped on top!

# Day 25

## Breakfast

### *Fat-bomb Iced Coffee*

*If you'd prefer to have a more substantial breakfast, you can absolutely substitute this recipe for another breakfast recipe from a previous day. Just make sure that it's a very low-carb recipe, as our day yesterday was quite high on the carb intake, by keto standards. To balance it out, we are having a really light carb day today.*

Servings: 2

Time: approximately 10 minutes

### Nutritional info:

- Calories: 310
- Fat: 30 grams
- Carbs: 6.5 grams
- Protein: 2 grams

### Ingredients:

- 3 tsp. instant coffee granules
- ¼ cup boiling water
- 1 cup ice, crushed
- 1 cup almond milk
- ½ cup cream
- 1 tsp. vanilla extract
- 1 Tbsp. flaxseed oil

### Directions:

1. Pour the boiling water over the coffee granules in a jug, stir to dissolve the coffee.
2. Add the ice, almond milk, cream, vanilla extract and flaxseed oil, stir to combine.
3. Serve!

# Lunch

## *Egg and Mayo Lettuce Wraps*

*Boiled eggs mixed with creamy mayo and a hint of sun-dried tomatoes, all wrapped in fresh, crisp lettuce leaves.*

Servings: 2

Time: approximately 20 minutes

## Nutritional info:

- Calories: 400
- Fat: 36.4 grams
- Carbs: 4.3 grams
- Protein: 13.7 grams

## Ingredients:

- 4 eggs, hard boiled, peeled and cut into small pieces
- 1/3 cup full-fat egg mayonnaise
- 5 sun-dried tomatoes, finely chopped
- 2 Tbsp. fresh parsley, chopped
- Salt and pepper
- 8 fresh lettuce leaves (I use big iceberg lettuce leaves)

## Directions:

1. In a small bowl, stir together the eggs, mayonnaise, sun-dried tomatoes, parsley, salt and pepper.
2. Spoon the mixture into the center of each lettuce leaf and roll tightly.
3. Pack away for later or serve immediately!

# Dinner

## *Fried Rice (cauliflower and broccoli rice) with Eggs and Edamame*

*This fried rice is made with a mixture of cauliflower and broccoli, with eggs, soy sauce and edamame beans for extra texture and subtle flavor.*

Servings: 4

Time: approximately 25 minutes

## Nutritional info:

- Calories: 190
- Fat: 11.5 grams
- Carbs: 12 grams
- Protein: 10.6 grams

## Ingredients:

- 4 cups cauliflower
- 2 cups broccoli
- 2 Tbsp. olive oil
- 2 garlic cloves, finely chopped
- ½ cup shelled edamame beans
- 2 Tbsp. soy sauce
- 3 eggs, lightly beaten

## Directions:

1. Place the cauliflower and broccoli into a food processor and blitz until it resembles rice.
2. Drizzle the olive oil into a frying pan and place over a medium heat.
3. Once the oil is hot, add the cauliflower, broccoli, garlic, edamame beans and soy sauce, stir to combine, keep stirring as the veggies fry.
4. Once the veggies are golden, add the egg and stir into the veggies.
5. When the egg is just set, it's time to serve!
6. Enjoy.

# Day 26

## Breakfast

### *Vanilla Balls*

*These are like little truffles filled with coconut, vanilla, ground almonds and bound together with thick Greek yogurt. Store in the fridge and eat 2 of them for breakfast!*

Servings: makes 12 balls (2 balls per serving)

Time: approximately 15 minutes

## Nutritional info:

- Calories: 206
- Fat: 16.7 grams
- Carbs: 7.5 grams
- Protein: 7.2 grams

## Ingredients:

- 3 oz. desiccated coconut, toasted on a dry pan until golden
- 1 cup ground almonds
- 3 tsp. vanilla extract
- 1 cup Greek yogurt

## Directions:

1. Place all ingredients into a bowl and stir to combine.
2. Roll the mixture into 12 balls and lay on a baking tray.
3. Place the tray into the fridge to allow the balls to set for about an hour.
4. Keep stored in an airtight container in the fridge.
5. Enjoy!

# Lunch

## *Silken Tofu with Roasted Broccoli and Tangy Dressing*

*We are using silken tofu this time because of its unique, silky texture. I love the flavor broccoli takes on when it is roasted, and the tangy dressing just adds an extra dimension of flavor.*

Servings: 4

Time: approximately 35 minutes

## Nutritional info:

- Calories: 230
- Fat: 17 grams
- Carbs: 10 grams
- Protein: 9 grams

## Ingredients:

- 2 cups broccoli
- 2 Tbsp. olive oil
- ¼ cup almonds, roughly chopped
- Salt and pepper
- 10 oz. silken tofu, cut into chunks
- 4 Tbsp. soy sauce
- 1 Tbsp. sesame oil
- Juice of 2 lemons

## Directions:

1. Preheat the oven to 400 degrees Fahrenheit and line a baking tray with baking paper.
2. Place the broccoli onto the baking tray, drizzle with olive oil salt and pepper.
3. Place the tray into the oven and bake for approximately 30 minutes or until golden and slightly crispy on the ends.

4. While the broccoli is baking, marinate the tofu: place the tofu into a medium-sized bowl and add the soy sauce, sesame oil and lemon juice, gently stir to combine, leave to marinate for 10 minutes.
5. After 10 minutes, place a non-stick frying pan over a medium heat.
6. Once the pan is hot, add the tofu and all of the sauce to the pan, fry the tofu until golden on both sides.
7. Serve the broccoli and tofu piled up on a plate or shallow bowl.
8. Enjoy!

# Dinner

## *Veggie Fritters with Fresh Mozzarella*

*These veggie fritters are slightly gooey on the inside, but crispy and golden on the outside. Served with soft, creamy, fresh mozzarella and a drizzle of olive oil and lemon juice.*

Servings: 4

Time: approximately 30 minutes

### Nutritional info:

- Calories: 380
- Fat: 30 grams
- Carbs: 16 grams
- Protein: 14 grams

### Ingredients:

- 1 carrot, grated
- 2 zucchinis, grated
- 1 small sweet potato, grated (about 1 cup)
- 2 eggs
- ½ cup ground almonds
- Salt and pepper
- Olive oil for frying
- 6 oz. fresh mozzarella
- Olive oil for drizzling
- Juice of 1 lemon

### Directions:

- Place the carrot, zucchini, sweet potato, egg, ground almonds, salt and pepper into a medium-sized bowl and stir to combine.
- Drizzle some olive oil into a non-stick pan and place over a medium heat.
- Once the oil is hot, drop spoonful-sized dollops of fritter mixture onto the hot surface and fry on both sides until golden.
- Serve the fritters with fresh mozzarella, olive oil and lemon juice.

# Day 27

## Breakfast

### *Overnight Chia Chocolate Pudding*

*Fiber-packed chia seeds soaked overnight in cream and coconut milk, with cocoa powder for a chocolate hit to start the day.*

Servings: 2

Time: approximately 10 minutes to prepare, overnight to set

**Nutritional info:**

- Calories: 360
- Fat: 31 grams
- Carbs: 14 grams
- Protein: 8 grams

**Ingredients:**

- 4 Tbsp. chia seeds
- 1 cup coconut milk
- ½ cup heavy cream
- 1 Tbsp. cocoa powder
- A few drops of stevia to sweeten to your taste

**Directions:**

1. Mix all ingredients in a small bowl before transferring to two serving bowls.
2. Cover and place into the fridge until morning.
3. Eat straight out of the fridge!

# Lunch

## *Hasselback Pumpkin*

*Rows of incisions are cut into chunks of pumpkin so delicious toppings can seep through. Cheese, sundried tomatoes and garlic ooze into the sweet, soft pumpkin flesh.*

Servings: 2

Time: approximately 40 minutes

## Nutritional info:

- Calories: 370
- Fat: 17 grams
- Carbs: 17 grams
- Protein: 8 grams

## Ingredients:

- ½ small pumpkin, cut into 4 wedges
- 1 cup cheddar cheese, grated
- 10 sun-dried tomatoes, roughly chopped
- 4 garlic cloves, finely chopped
- 4 Tbsp. scallions, finely chopped
- 2 Tbsp. olive oil
- Salt and pepper

## Directions:

1. Preheat the oven to 420 degrees Fahrenheit and line a baking tray with baking paper.
2. Cut deep incisions into the pumpkin wedges and separate the pieces out, so that there are gaps between the incisions.
3. In a small bowl, mix together the cheese, sun-dried tomatoes, garlic, scallions, olive oil, salt and pepper.
4. Lay the pumpkin onto the lined tray.

5. Spoon the cheese mixture over each piece of pumpkin and press the mixture into the incisions.
6. Bake in the preheated oven for approximately 35 minutes or until the pumpkin is soft and the cheese is golden and melted!

# Dinner

## *Mushroom Puttanesca with Parmesan and Crème Fraiche*

*Instead of replacing spaghetti with something else, I've decided to just make the puttanesca sauce! Once it is dished-up with parmesan and creme fraiche you'll hardly miss the pasta.*

Servings: 4

Time: approximately 30 minutes

## Nutritional info:

- Calories: 250
- Fat: 21 grams
- Carbs: 7.5 grams
- Protein: 6.3 grams

## Ingredients:

- 2 Tbsp. olive oil
- 2 cups mushrooms, sliced
- 2 cups canned chopped tomatoes
- 3 Tbsp. capers
- 16 black olives, pitted, roughly chopped
- 2 tsp. dried chili flakes
- Salt and pepper
- 2 oz. grated Parmesan cheese
- 4 Tbsp. creme fraiche

## Directions:

1. Drizzle the olive oil into a frying pan and place over a medium heat.
2. Once the oil is hot, add the mushrooms and stir as they soften and become golden.
3. Add the tomatoes, capers, olives, chili flakes, salt and pepper, stir to combine.
4. Leave to simmer on a low heat for approximately 20 minutes, adding a dash of water if the sauce appears to be drying out.
5. Serve with a generous grating of parmesan cheese and a tablespoon of creme fraiche per serving.

# Day 28

## Breakfast

### *Cranberry, Yogurt and Almond Milk Smoothie*

*Cranberries might seem like an odd ingredient to use all of a sudden, but they are great for bladder health and make for a refreshing change from other berries. However, if you cannot get your hands on them, just use blueberries or raspberries instead!*

Servings: 2

Time: approximately 10 minutes

Nutritional info:

- Calories: 160
- Fat: 5.7 grams
- Carbs: 17.7 grams
- Protein: 11.5 grams

## Ingredients:

- 1 cup cranberries, fresh or frozen
- 1 cup Greek yogurt
- 1 cup almond milk
- 2 Tbsp. flaxseed oil
- 1 cup ice

## Directions:

1. Place all ingredients into a blender and blitz until smooth
2. Serve!

# Lunch

## *Poached Eggs with Pea, Spinach and Cream Cheese Mash*

*A take on the classic smashed peas. On the keto diet, peas should be eaten in very small amounts, so we are using spinach and cream cheese to fill the dish out.*

Servings: 2

Time: approximately 20 minutes

### Nutritional info:

- Calories: 500
- Fat: 40 grams
- Carbs: 11.5 grams
- Protein: 21 grams

### Ingredients:

- 1 Tbsp. olive oil
- 2 garlic cloves, finely chopped
- 2 cups spinach, roughly chopped
- ½ cup peas (fresh or frozen)
- 5 oz. cream cheese
- 4 eggs
- Salt and pepper

### Directions:

1. Drizzle the olive oil into a frying pan and place over a medium heat.
2. Once the oil is hot, add the garlic, spinach, peas, salt and pepper.
3. Stir as the spinach wilts and the peas cook, smash the peas with your spoon.
4. Turn the heat off and add the cream cheese, stir to combine.
5. Boil 2 inches of water in a pot or frying pan.
6. Once the water is simmering, crack the eggs into the water and poach until the egg whites turn from clear to opaque.

7. Divide the pea mixture between two plates.
8. Use a slotted spoon to take the eggs out of the water, place them on top of the pea mixture.
9. Sprinkle with salt and pepper.
10. Eat up!

# Dinner

## *Fried Kale Parcels*

*For dinner tonight, we are wrapping egg, cheese, veggies and nuts in kale leaves. Then, we fry our little parcels in olive oil!*

Servings: 4

Time: approximately 30 minutes

### Nutritional info:

- Calories: 325
- Fat: 21 grams
- Carbs: 6.2 grams
- Protein: 11.2 grams

### Ingredients:

- 4 eggs
- 1 cup grated cheddar cheese
- 1 leek, finely sliced
- ¼ walnuts, roughly chopped
- 1 cup mushrooms, sliced
- Salt and pepper
- 8 kale leaves
- 3 Tbsp. olive oil
- 8 toothpicks

### Directions:

1. In a medium-sized bowl, mix together the eggs, grated cheese, leek, walnuts, mushrooms, salt and pepper.
2. Drizzle the olive oil into a frying pan and place over a medium-high heat.
3. While the pan is heating up, fill the kale leaves: lay the kale leaves onto a board, spoon the egg mixture into the center of each leaf.
4. Wrap the leaves tightly around the mixture and secure closed with a toothpick.
5. Place the parcels into the hot oil and fry on both sides until crispy.
6. Enjoy while hot, warm or cold!

# Day 29

## Breakfast

### *Blueberry Muffins*

*These blueberry muffins are made with cream cheese, ground almonds, and of course... blueberries! They are sweet, soft and very satisfying to munch on for breakfast. Since they are so low in carbs and calories, a single serving is TWO muffins!*

Servings: 6

Time: approximately 30 minutes

**Nutritional info:**

- Calories: 255
- Fat: 20 grams
- Carbs: 12 grams
- Protein: 8.5 grams

**Ingredients:**

- 2 eggs
- 6 oz. cream cheese
- ½ cup heavy cream
- 1 cup ground almonds
- 1 tsp. baking powder
- 2 cups blueberries

**Directions:**

1. Preheat the oven to 375 degrees Fahrenheit and grease a 12-hole muffin pan with butter, or simply place a paper cupcake case into each hole.
2. Place the eggs, cream cheese and cream into a medium-sized bowl and whisk to combine.
3. Add the almonds and baking powder, fold into the egg mixture.
4. Gently fold the blueberries into the mixture.
5. Spoon the mixture into the greased muffin holes.
6. Bake for approximately 25 minutes or until golden and set.
7. Eat two for breakfast!

# Lunch

## *Eggplant Fries with Garlic Mayonnaise*

*For lunch, we are feasting on fries made from eggplants, dipped in creamy garlic mayo!*

Servings: 2

Time: approximately 25 minutes

### Nutritional info:

- Calories: 565
- Fat: 51 grams
- Carbs: 12.7 grams
- Protein: 16.5 grams

### Ingredients:

- 3 eggplants, cut into fries (long, square batons)
- 2 eggs, gently beaten with a fork
- ½ cup grated Parmesan cheese
- ½ cup full-fat egg mayonnaise
- 1 garlic clove, minced or finely chopped
- Salt and pepper
- Olive oil for frying

### Directions:

1. Dip the eggplant batons into the beaten egg, then transfer to the grated Parmesan cheese, repeat until all of the fries have been coated in egg and Parmesan cheese.
2. Drizzle some olive oil into a frying pan and place over a medium-high heat.
3. While the oil is heating up, make the garlic mayo: mix together the mayonnaise and the minced garlic in a small bowl.
4. When the oil is hot, very carefully place a single layer of eggplant fries onto the hot pan surface and fry on all sides until golden.
5. Dip the fries into your garlic mayo and enjoy!

# Dinner

## *Fresh Herb, Mozzarella and Roasted Veggie Salad*

*Fresh herbs in a salad provide fragrance and a world of varying flavors from sweet to spicy. Again, I've chosen fresh mozzarella to go with this salad, as I just cannot get past that magical creaminess!*

Servings: 4

Time: approximately 35 minutes

### Nutritional info:

- Calories: 300
- Fat: 20 grams
- Carbs: 16 grams
- Protein: 12 grams

### Ingredients:

- 2 bell peppers, seeds removed, sliced
- 1 cup sweet potato, cubes
- 1 red onion, roughly chopped
- 3 Tbsp. olive oil
- Salt and pepper
- 1 cup mixed fresh leafy herbs: basil, mint, mustard, cilantro etc. whatever you've got in the garden
- 6 cups lettuce, roughly chopped
- 8 oz. fresh mozzarella, torn or chopped into rough chunks
- 2 tsp. apple cider vinegar

### Directions:

1. Preheat the oven to 400 degrees Fahrenheit and line a baking tray with baking paper.
2. Lay the bell peppers, sweet potatoes and red onion onto the tray.
3. Drizzle with olive oil, salt and pepper.

4. Place into the oven and bake for approximately 30 minutes or until golden and cooked through.
5. Place the cooked veggies into a salad bowl and add the herbs, lettuce and mozzarella.
6. Drizzle the apple cider vinegar over the salad before serving!

# Day 30

## Breakfast

### *Yoghurt, Berry and Cream Whip*

*Whipped cream mixed with yogurt and dotted with fresh berries. A drizzle of healthy flaxseed oil finishes the dish off with a dose of good... no, GREAT fat.*

Servings: 2

Time: approximately 10 minutes

## Nutritional info:

- Calories: 490
- Fat: 40 grams
- Carbs: 15 grams
- Protein: 20 grams

## Ingredients:

- 2 cups Greek yogurt
- ¾ cup heavy cream, whipped
- ½ cup mixed berries
- 1 Tbsp, flaxseed oil

## Directions:

1. Mix together the yogurt, whipped cream and berries.
2. Spoon the mixture into two serving dishes.
3. Drizzle with flaxseed oil.
4. Ready to eat!

# Lunch

## *Broccoli, Leek and Cheddar Soup*

*For our last day, we are having a creamy, cheesy, veggie-filled soup. More broccoli, more leeks and more cheddar!*

Servings: 4

Time: approximately 30 minutes

## Nutritional info:

- Calories: 220
- Fat: 9 grams
- Carbs: 12.5 grams
- Protein: 5 grams

## Ingredients:

- 2 cups broccoli
- 2 leeks, roughly chopped
- 2 garlic cloves, roughly chopped
- 1 cup cheddar cheese
- 2 cups vegetable broth (stock)
- 1/3 cup cream
- Salt and pepper

## Directions:

1. Place the broccoli, leeks, garlic, cheese, broth, salt and pepper into a large pot and place over a medium heat.
2. Bring to the boil and leave to boil for approximately 20 minutes or until the veggies are very soft.
3. With a handheld blender, blend the soup until very smooth.
4. Stir the cream into the soup before serving, and sprinkle with an extra dash of salt and pepper.
5. Enjoy nice and hot!

# Dinner

## *Baked Brie with Kale Chips*

*The last dinner is something a bit more special and luxurious. It does seem more like a starter or snack, but because of the high fat content, it is very satiating! Creamy brie, crunchy walnuts, and crispy kale chips.*

Servings: 4

Time: approximately 30 minutes

## Nutritional info:

- Calories: 385
- Fat: 35 grams
- Carbs: 6 grams
- Protein: 15.5 grams

## Ingredients:

- 9 oz. wheel of brie (or the closest you can find to 9 oz)
- 2 Tbsp. olive oil
- 2 Tbsp. walnuts
- 4 cups kale, cut into "chip" size
- 1 Tbsp. coconut oil
- Salt and pepper

## Directions:

1. Preheat the oven to 375 degrees Fahrenheit and grease a small baking dish with olive oil.
2. Place the brie into the greased baking dish and drizzle the olive oil and walnuts over the top.
3. Place the dish into the oven and bake the brie for about 12 minutes, or until soft and oozy.

4. After you take the brie out of the oven, keep the oven on and prepare the kale chips: spread the kale onto a paper-lined baking tray, drizzle with olive oil, salt and pepper.
5. Place the tray into the oven and bake for 5-10 minutes or until the kale chips are crisp but NOT burnt.
6. You can eat the kale chips alone, alongside the baked brie, or you can spread some of the baked brie onto a kale chip and eat them together!
7. ENJOY!

# Conclusion

I hope that after these 30 delicious days you are feeling satisfied, inspired and energized! If you are a temporary vegetarian and you are planning on introducing meat back into your life, you can adjust these recipes accordingly. Perhaps you could allocate 2 "meaty" dinners a week, so you're still getting the benefits of meat without foregoing the benefits of a diet which is light on the meat, and heavy on the fresh produce.

Remember to add healthy, low-carb stacks to your day during these 30 days, so you are getting enough calories to stay strong and alert.


Happy cooking!

Made in the USA
San Bernardino, CA
25 June 2018